GOD IN CHICAGO

ALSO BY DEJI KOMOLAFE

Class of Hope and Change: A Walk with Millennials

God In Chicago

A JOURNEY THROUGH CITY STREETS AND SPIRITUAL BELIEFS

DEJI KOMOLAFE

OverPond

CHICAGO

Copyright © 2021 by Deji Komolafe.

All rights reserved. No part of this publication may be reproduced, distributed or transmitted in any form or by any means, including photocopying, recording, or other electronic or mechanical methods, without the prior written permission of the publisher, except in the case of brief quotations embodied in critical reviews and certain other noncommercial uses permitted by copyright law.

For permission requests, write to the publisher at the address below.

OverPond Media
PO Box 876
Chicago, IL 60680
info@overpondmedia.com

Cover Design by Beetiful Book Covers
Cover features the sculpture *Looking Up* by Tom Friedman. 2015, Burnham Park, Chicago.

Copyediting by WordWiser Ink LLC
Book Layout ©2017 BookDesignTemplates.com

Ordering Information:
Quantity sales. Special discounts are available on quantity purchases by corporations, associations, and others. For details, contact the "Special Sales Department" at the address above.

God In Chicago: A Journey through City Streets and Spiritual Beliefs/ Deji Komolafe -- 1st ed.
Paperback ISBN: 978-1-7363104-0-3
ebook ISBN 978-1-7363104-1-0

To JBC, a space where I felt known

and

To ACOG, a space where I felt at home

"I was a stranger, and you invited me in."

Matthew 25:35

CONTENTS

EXCELLENCE {63RD & DORCHESTER}	*1*
CARING {OGDEN & AVERS}	*5*
ANTICIPATION {45TH & PRINCETON}	*9*
PRESENCE {51ST & KEELER}	*13*
PRACTICAL {AUSTIN & LAKE}	*17*
BEAUTIFUL {95TH & EGGLESTON}	*21*
NOURISHED {WASHINGTON & PARKSIDE}	*25*
LONGSUFFERING {114TH & CORLISS}	*29*
LOVE {KEDZIE & ALBANY}	*35*
TIMELESS {37TH & WENTWORTH}	*39*
RECOVERY {GRAND & HAMLIN}	*45*
CLARITY {78TH & RACINE}	*49*
EVERYWHERE {ROOSEVELT & TRIPP}	*55*
TEMPTATION {23RD & MICHIGAN}	*61*
AWAKE {GARFIELD & PAULINA}	*67*
FIRE {WABASH & ERIE}	*71*
LEVELS {38TH & INDIANA}	*77*
ANCESTRY {CLARK & LASALLE}	*81*
CARE {NORTH & RUTHERFORD}	*87*
AMBASSADOR {WASHINGTON & ALBANY}	*93*
RUNNING {CICERO & BELMONT}	*99*
RESTART {24TH & WABASH}	*105*
LOST {RACINE & ADAMS}	*111*
DEATH {JACKSON & LARAMIE}	*115*
WORDS {HOLLYWOOD & GLENWOOD}	*121*
FAMILY {79TH & WABASH}	*127*
PERSONAL {WASHINGTON & KILDARE}	*133*
GATEWAY {KEDZIE & MONTROSE}	*139*
CHANGE {CHICAGO & GREEN}	*145*
THANKS {62ND & THROOP}	*151*
REJOICE {CERMAK & CANALPORT}	*155*
TEARS {79TH & COLES}	*161*
OBEY {ARMITAGE & ORCHARD}	*167*
HOLIDAYS {49TH & KING DRIVE}	*173*
COMPLETION {56TH & WOODLAWN}	*179*
ACKNOWLEDGEMENTS	*185*

PREFACE

I love music festivals. Well, I loved music festivals. The jubilant, multi-day gatherings of beautiful music and beautiful people were one of the countless expressions of communal humanity that were halted in 2020 by the global pandemic of COVID-19. As I make the final edits to this manuscript, it doesn't look like anyone will be partying en masse anytime soon.

There is something liberating about being able to meld seamlessly into a larger crowd - whether by yourself or with a group of loved ones - and just *be*. Sometimes, it's nice to be able to experience joy without having to connect to anyone else if you don't want to, or to connect with others at a level that works for you.

However, there is something distinctly powerful about gathering in spaces where you are known by name. Spaces where people expect to see you, and ask about you when they don't. Spaces where you have connected with people in a deeply transparent and authentic manner. Spaces where you are wanted. Spaces where you are needed. I am a product of such spaces.

Despite the widely held belief among Americans in the narratives of rugged individualism, individual genius, and personal exceptionalism; 2020 proved that we don't just like to gather with others, we *need* to. Many people were willing to risk their lives for the opportunity to party, protest, play, and/or pray together.

Americans have spent the first two decades of the 21st century collectively drifting away from houses of prayer and praise as primary spaces for friendship, community, meaning, and identity. And though we increasingly look to platforms, politics, and personalities to provide a central organizing force for connecting with others about the things that matter to us, 2020 exposed the side effects and limitations of this approach, and revealed that many of us still long for something deeper, and higher.

◆

You can't go home again[1].

Author Tom Wolfe brought this often-referenced thought to American culture 80 years ago. And for most of us, it still rings true. Things are never exactly the same as you remember them. Places change. People change. We change. *Home* changes.

After a decade away, I recently had the opportunity to return home. I returned to the city of my birth, and to the place where the foundation of my faith was formed. I have been through a lot since I lived in Chicago. The city has been through a lot since I left. I never

[1] Wolfe, Thomas. You Can't Go Home Again. New York: Harper & Bros, 1940.

left my faith, but I see it differently now. The communities of faith across the city's neighborhoods never left, but I look at them differently now.

Some of my longest friendships, some of my most important mentors, the inspiration for my career choice, my first employer, a significant portion of my formative experiences as a youth, my understanding of race and class in this city, the community of women who supported and nourished my mother as she found herself having to raise me and my brother largely by herself....all of these cornerstones of my life were molded in these spaces.

Having moved in and around communities of faith for over three decades, I am neither objective in my observations, nor oblivious in my opinions about them. I have intentionally chosen to share the stories about my year-long journey visiting 35 faith communities in Chicago during 2017 in a manner that is stripped of the packaging & pageantry, labels & titles, divisions & denominations that matter to fewer people now than they did when they were created.

Is there anything here?   *What about Chicago?*
Is there anything left?   *What about God?*

The people assembled in the faith communities I visited were not there by force. Only a small percentage of them were being financially compensated for attending these weekly gatherings with their fellow community members. For the majority of these people, given that Sunday mornings are often precious and rare times of rest, it was not in their general economic interest to get out of bed, get dressed, and spend some money on gas or public transportation to be a part of a fellowship of like-minded individuals.

Hopefully, this book will challenge the misconceptions about these spaces and celebrate the humanity of the people who gather in them.

This book was written in hopes that people who may be unfamiliar with these norms (and/or confused by the large swath of American society influenced by them) will find a bridge to walk with me as I consider the central questions of life, spirituality, and our beliefs about God.

I invite you to open yourself to whatever emotions and thoughts are inspired or provoked by this journey. To help, I offer the following series of meditations as a spiritual tapas buffet. Hopefully, your mental taste buds are activated by the ideas and topics engaged.

PLEASE NOTE: The words in the following meditations of this preface are mine, and do not necessarily represent the opinions, beliefs, musings, or queries of any of the institutions I visited for this book.

CHURCH BOY

Boy, you gotta go to church, again?!

                                                Boy, get yo butt to church!

Boy, why
you still going to that church?!

                                        Boy, you know why
                                        we going up to that church!

Boy, there you go
on that church sh*t again

                                          Boy, you know
                                        we back on that church sh*t

Boys don't go to church
if they want to become real men

                                        Boys go to church
                              because they want to become real men

Church is no place for a man

                                    Church is the first place for a man

Man, I don't know how you go

                                    Man, I don't know how you don't

WHERE EVIL LIVES

Evil doesn't live here
Oh no
evil lives

                Over There

In history books
and black and white
documentaries
in far-away places
in the minds
of other people

                Never Here

'Cuz we believe
in freedom
in law and order
in equality
in humanity

                in God

I DON'T HATE YOU

(after Marianne Williamson[1])

My deepest fear is not
that you are inadequate.

My deepest fear is that
I won't mind my business.

It is not your light,
but our darkness that most frightens us.
We ask ourselves,
"What kind of man am I
if I get called *gorgeous and fabulous*?"

You are a child of God.
Your playing small does not serve God.
There is nothing enlightened about shrinking you
so that we won't feel insecure talking to God around you.

And as we let our own light shine,
we consciously acknowledge that
other people don't need permission to do the same.

As we are liberated from our own fear,
your presence intentionally liberates others.

---

[1] Marianne Williamson, *A Return to Love,* (HarperCollins, 1992)

DON'T GO THERE

One of the surprisingly difficult parts of this project was figuring out where I could go. God might be open to everyone, but God's people? That's another story entirely.

To talk about Chicago, and not talk about race, would be malpractice. To talk about spiritual or religious beliefs, and not talk about the societal belief that darker bodies are inferior or inhuman ones, would be malpractice.

So, one thing you should know - one thing I knew - was that I could not simply visit *any* spiritual space that interested me, fade into the background, observe, engage, and experience a new spiritual community in good will and good faith.

Bodies like mine are routinely met with caution, reservation, fear, curiosity, suspicion, and occasionally, hate. So my answer to the question: *"So, why are you here?"* cannot simply be *"I came to hear about God."* In certain spiritual spaces in this city, I would need to receive pre-approval. To arrive unannounced would be a disturbance to the social order of that faith community.

So, I went where I could. Where I could *be*. Where I could be nonthreatening. Where I could be welcomed. Where I could be tolerated. Where I could be accepted. Where I could be trusted. Where I could be understood. Where I could be *seen*. Where I could be heard. Where I could be loved.

SEX ED PARABLES

If your child knows The Word but does not know their body, you ain't doin' it right.

◊

If the act that brought them into existence is treated with shame and secrecy, how will your child learn how to live in freedom and truth?

◊

If you think, *"well my parents didn't talk to me about it, and I turned out okay"*...you might not be okay.

◊

If you don't see your house or God's House as a safe space for them to learn about it, do you trust the internet and their peers more?

◊

Unprotected sex is very risky.
Abstinence that is protected by fear and shame is very risky.

◊

At what age should education about sex begin?
At what age should education about sex end?

◊

What do you think will happen if kids are taught about sexual identities? What do you think will happen if they are not?

◊

Should the people who talk to you about God be the same people who talk to you about sex?
Should the people who talk to you about sex be the same people who talk to you about God?

GOD BLESS YOU

Who Does God Bless?

☐ Lots of people ☐ Only good people ☐ Everyone

☐ Only people like me ☐ Only me ☐ No one

Why Does God Bless?

☐ Because I earned it ☐ Because I deserve it ☐ Out of love

☐ Out of pity ☐ Out of boredom ☐ Because I asked

What Does God Bless?

☐ My stuff ☐ My soul ☐ My body

☐ My country ☐ My goals ☐ My family & friends

THE MAN NEXT TO THE MAN

To the Man of God who keeps his small church open in the shadow of another man's megachurch:

I get it. Although we all like to think of ourselves as servants, there is some competition and pride involved. It's hard to be Blockbuster when Netflix blows up. No one wants to be Blackberry, everyone wants to be Apple. We don't remember the remember the team who loses the championship. Sure, the runner-up on *American Idol* is still famous, but it's not the same, is it?

In a city this big, with big dreams, and big possibilities, and big vacant lots across the street, and big unemployment, and big boys shooting big guns, and big banks investing big money everywhere you are not, and big enforcement of big laws that send all those big boys to big prisons for big payments to big companies...can we afford to have big men with big egos?

Thousands of people, every week, walk by a building you own. They have all sorts of needs, and all sorts of wants, and all sorts of questions, and all sorts of interests, and all sorts of things to do after the benediction.

Can you serve them without preaching to them?

Respectfully,
A Passerby

MISSION TRIPS

"A team from There is coming Here.
They are coming to help us.
Because we need help.
They do too,
but they don't talk about that.
We pray God would use them.
We pray God would use us.
So we both are changed.
They will only be here for a week,
so we will give them meaningful things to do.
Hopefully they will remember their experience,
the next time they vote for their leaders."

◊

"We prayerfully considered it.
We just wanted to be used by God.
So we sent a team.
We were only there for a week,
but they were so happy to see us.
To see the smiles on the kids' faces.
They are so happy, even with so little.
And we have so much,
it makes you grateful for what you have.
I learned so much from them,
I would definitely go back."

THE BUILDING FUND

We funded buildings
in neighborhoods
we can no longer
afford to live in.

Why do we fund buildings?

We funded buildings
in neighborhoods
where we don't own
businesses.

What kind of buildings should we fund?

We built funds
in banks
that
foreclosed
in neighborhoods
we built.

Where should our funds be built?

We built funds
and now
we have none.

How can we fund buildings?

LOST IN TRANSLATION

A Faith Personality Quiz

1) "The Bible was originally written in English."
(Disagree = 1 point , Agree = 5 points)

2) "God is European."
(Agree = 10 points , Disagree = 2 points)

3) "America is God's chosen country."
(Of course! = 8 points, It's Possible = 6 points, No Way! = 4 points)

4) "Some countries are cursed by God."
(Ridiculous! = 1 point, Possible = 4 points, Obviously! = 8 points)

5) "Each human life on Earth is equally valued by God."
(Agree = 2 point , Not Sure = 5 points, Disagree = 10 points)

6) "God loves me more than some other people."
(Ridiculous! = 1 point, Possibly = 4 points, Obviously! = 8 points)

7) "People who believe in God should be financially rich."
(No = 1 point, Why? = 4 points, Why not? = 6 points, Yes = 10 points)

JUDGE THIS BOOK BY ITS COVER

I chose the sky,
because it's big
and blue.
Blue is my color,
and Big is the first word that comes to mind
when I think about God.

I chose the sky
because it is high
above everyone,
whether they can see it
or not.

I chose the sky
because it is where
sun and rain
come from,
and life
needs both.

I chose the sky
because whether
I am happy,
or overwhelmed,
my hands stretch towards it.

EXCELLENCE
{63RD & DORCHESTER}

I began my journey here because this was one of two places that shaped my understanding of God during my teens and early 20s. This has always been a place where I could get my head right. When my life's road brought me back to the Chicago area a few months ago, it only made sense to start my search for God in this place.

This place is a cathedral to God. The way stadiums are cathedrals to sports. The way skyscrapers are cathedrals to capitalism. This place is designed to make a statement, about God and about the community that assembles here every week.

And statements matter. Especially for this neighborhood, which borders the campus of an elite university that trains people to run the world, but also borders a community that is fighting to protect its youth from running the streets.

It's obvious that presentation matters to the people here. Although they celebrated New Year's Eve here just nine hours earlier, this doesn't look like it. This is not a leftover celebration. They are dressed for this morning's gathering. I see the excellence of God in their decoration of this space, and of themselves.

> Surrounded by people who present themselves with excellence,
> and who care for this space with excellence,
> I am ready to hear something about an excellent God.

> ***"When you look at your neighbor,***
> ***you're looking at a victorious life."***

"When you <u>look</u> at your neighbor..." Not, "Look at your phone." Not , "Look up to the heavens." Look at your neighbor. Look at this person randomly seated next to you on a padded bench in the auditorium balcony. Look at them. At 9am. On a cold Sunday. On New Year's Day.

When I think about where God might be found on this morning, in the eyes of whoever happens to be seated next to me would not be my first thought!

Yet this is exactly the kind of message I will need for the journey ahead. I can't get caught up looking at neighborhood maps, police statistics, or socioeconomic labels.

'I need to look at people.

"*...look at your <u>neighbor</u>...*" The speaker's use of the word "neighbor" suggests that there are both benefits and responsibilities that come from my interaction with the other people gathered here. This framework asks me to think about my relationship to those around me differently than I normally would, say on a subway train or in a coffee shop.

"...*look at your neighbor...*" According to the Merriam-Webster Dictionary, 'your' means "relating to you, especially as possessor." Some things are yours because you selected or claimed them. Some things are yours because they were assigned to you.

In the speaker's framework, "your neighbor" does not just include the neighbors who I know and like. The people I chose to sit next to. "Your neighbor" includes the people I do not know, and may not like. The people I was destined to sit next to.

It asks me to see the people next to me in their full humanity. To see all that they are, to see all that they are not. It reminds my neighbor to do likewise when they look at me.

"*...you're looking at a victorious life.*" This is a bold statement of aspiration and expectation, especially given the level of sustained suffering and struggle endured in the streets to the south and west of this space. I would not have to move far from my seat on this bench to find someone who has not been personally impacted by the parade of tragedies visited upon the residents of the surrounding neighborhoods in recent years.

The speaker defined victorious, "*not by what you've gone through...but by how you came out.*" In this sense, someone who has endured and survived has achieved a victory. Your neighbor's presence, your own presence, is evidence of a victorious life.

The speaker's words challenge me to re-evaluate the widely held belief that being victorious at life depends of what I have acquired, accumulated, and attracted. The speaker is asking the audience to see our neighbors as winners because they are still here, despite all they have been through.

Good words to start the new year.

CARING

{OGDEN & AVERS}

I haven't seen anything quite like this from a community of faith. Along this stretch of Ogden Avenue lies a mini-campus of buildings owned and managed by, or affiliated with, the members of this faith community; created to serve the residents of the surrounding communities.

There's a building called Hope House. Another one called Perkins Center. There's a learning center, a health center, an agape chapel, and a fitness center. Even the indie coffee shop on the corner might be part of this impressive hub of activity on the west side.

◊

There were around 30 people inside the main building when I arrived. There were about 300 chairs arranged around a short square platform like a boxing match is about to take place.

The building - an old-school gymnasium with wood beam rafters - has a comfortable and low-key vibe. This is a come-as-you-are kind of place. No one here is wearing a suit. There are no expensive cars parked in front of the entrance.

There are a few white families in attendance today, which normally would not be noteworthy; but I couldn't help but be reminded that we were in the same Chicago neighborhood where Dr. Martin Luther King Jr. lived with his family in the summer of 1966. I was reminded that during this Chicago Freedom Movement summer, Dr. King encountered two of the most violent and hateful displays of resistance to his work. One in a neighborhood 3 miles to the west of this building, and another in a neighborhood 8 miles south.

As I watched more people enter the building, it's obvious that these people know each other. They are not simply co-located in this space, they are communing with one another.

As the event begins, six women take the small square stage and prepared to lead the audience in a series of songs. One of the women puts her finger up to her lips, motioning to the toddler in the front row.

◊

About 30 minutes later, the prayer and praise session began. People from various points on the socio-economic spectrum walked up to one of two microphones placed at opposite corners of the center stage, and shared with the audience what was going on in their lives.

There were so many people dealing with medical/health challenges, either in their own bodies, or in the bodies of their family members. The differences in the appearance of human bodies have been used to justify so much evil on this planet; yet the similarity in the functioning our bodies - especially when they stop functioning - was the commonality uniting the audience during this session.

◊

Today, the speaker had chosen to talk about the concept of love. The following line from his talk stood out to me:

"Love is the essence of who we are.
If you don't feel love, we haven't been doing our job right."

What a powerful concept. The idea that the test of whether any community is operating in love is *not* whether they talk about loving people; it is whether someone entering the community can feel the love. This kind of mindset raises the bar for communities of people who claim to be talking to God, listening to God, and following God's plan.

- What would my life look like if loving people was my job?
- What would our families look like if loving each other was the primary motivation behind our actions?
- What would our businesses, schools, and government institutions look like if loving people was a main component of their mission?
- What would this country look like if loving people was as American as speaking your mind?

ANTICIPATION
{45TH & PRINCETON}

As I drive up Princeton Street, I couldn't help but think about the cruel irony of the street's name. A name it shares with one of America's oldest institutions of privilege, power, and wealth. This street runs as a kind of middle rail between the Dan Ryan Expressway and the Norfolk Southern & Metra train tracks.

If you were doing one of those sports pre-game feature profiles of a young athlete from the "mean streets" of Chicago's south side, the landscape of this street on this morning is the video footage you would see: gray skies, bordered up homes, vacant lots, few businesses.

Across the street, a flock of over 50 geese have assembled in the outfield shared by two opposing baseball diamonds.

As I walk into the building, I was struck by the unique way the auditorium's design creates an intimate environment for the audience. The stage was open and close to the seats. The balcony seemed to be closer to the stage and the main level than I've seen at other places.

As I waited for the event to begin, I watched the comfortable conversation between pairs and small groups of people as they made their way to their preferred rows.

Next to me, a young boy politely steps into a conversation between two women discussing pre-kindergarten registration:

"Can you please stop talking to my mommy?"

Both women laugh. This child looks comfortable in this space. He has been here before many times. He recognizes faces, they recognize his. He seems cared for, and cared about. I think about who he will be 10 years from now, 20 years from now. Will this building still be a place where he is recognized, welcomed, loved, and cared for?

◊

The worship team began to perform a song with the chorus: *"I choose to be free."* This chorus seems to accurately describe the energy of the people around me.

Two times during this event, time was set aside for the audience to greet the people seated next to them - not simply with the customary handshake and *"Praise the Lord"* or *"God Bless You,"* but with a hug.

ANTICIPATION {45TH & PRINCETON}

In fact, between the hug greetings, and the *"Tap your neighbor"* interludes, this is a high-touch environment. A powerful experience in the context of the geographic and cultural communities who are served by this place.

Many people go a whole week without hearing a kind word spoken to them. Without seeing a smile directed toward them. Without the feel a non-sexual touch. You have to feel safe in your body and in your space to allow a stranger to touch you. You have to feel safe in your body and in your space to allow yourself to touch a stranger.

The people around me were clearly operating in both levels of safety. I wondered how many people in this neighborhood, in this city, or even in this country have experienced this kind of safety outside of their homes recently.

I thought about the walls we each have to construct around ourselves just to go out into the world. We build these walls to keep harm away from our minds, spirits, and bodies. We build walls so that we are not touched and harmed by the people and situations we may encounter. We build walls so that we don't accidentally hurt ourselves by trying to touch something - or someone - outside of our defined safe zone. Building walls is a necessary part of operating as a human in a society that is exponentially larger than the familial tribe we each come from.

Walls are also constructed by others to keep us out. Unless you are one of the few people who are both well-known *and* well-liked around the world, to most of the world's population, we are the stranger, the *other*, the external force they need to protect themselves from.

Because of this, most of us go through life both maintaining walls to get away from danger, and climbing over walls to get closer to resources and relationships. So when the main speaker came to the podium and announced that she would be talking about one of the most famous wall collapses in the history of the Judeo-Christian tradition, it was right in line with my current train of thought.

"If the wall is still up, what are you shouting about?"

Without going into the specific Biblical reference the speaker was discussing, I thought there were some profound revelations in her talk about anticipating God's actions.

"God wants you to see it done, while it is still undone...You have to envision the wall flat, 'cuz you have seven days to see the wall [still] standing up."

Seeing God helping you to overcome an obstacle that appears to be blocking your options, and believing your situation will improve when you have no evidence for that belief, is the definition of faith. It is also the difference between having faith and being optimistic.

- In how many situations in our lives do we actually exercise faith in God?
- Do we usually just wait until we can see a potential path to progress, and then exercise optimism in God?

The main speaker ended her talk by asking the audience to join hands as she shared her closing thought:

"Hold your neighbors' hands. Squeeze your neighbors' hands. When you know God can do something for you, you don't have to wait until there's a physical manifestation."

PRESENCE
{51ST & KEELER}

I did not have any pre-conceived ideas about what to expect as I pulled into the parking lot behind an elementary school and in the shadow of the Orange Line elevated tracks. Yet I would be lying if I said I wasn't a little surprised when I walked into the well-lit open lobby and saw an information kiosk in the center, a merchandise booth in the corner to my right, and a 4-5 table coffee shop on my left.

It was...professional. Like going to a hotel ballroom for a seminar or conference. But it was also familiar, and definitely had a come-as-you-are vibe. There was a signature book for first-time visitors placed at each aisle as you enter the auditorium.

As I waited for the event to begin, I flipped through the brochure I'd been given, and watched the scattered small groups of people chatting in the auditorium. In the upper right hand corner of the informational brochure, I noticed a small box of text titled *Weekly Budget*. Listed underneath the title was the organization's budget for the week, and the amount of money they had raised from donations the previous week.

This is the first place I've been, so far, that mentioned how much they spend. It seems to be an effort to build trust through transparency. I wonder what led to the decision to share this information with visiting guests and committed members alike.

That got me to thinking about how we try to gain the trust and confidence of people in our personal lives. How often do we start by sharing something as personal as how we spend our money?

I wonder how many companies, government agencies, schools, nonprofit organizations, or social clubs build trust with newcomers by sharing the specific dollar amounts they spend each week?

I think, on some level, this small disclosure had an effect on me. I felt better about the projectors, soundstage, screens, and modern decor in this auditorium; which were a contrast to the nondescript and understated exterior of this building and the buildings on the surrounding blocks.

◊

Sometime in the middle of the event, after the singing, the speaker said to the audience:

*"If you are in the community of faith, you're on the winning side...
Give three people around you a high-five to let them know they are
in the right place, at the right time."*

These were interesting and powerful declarations. The speaker was contending that simply by being in the company of other people who believe, you would be on the winning side.

We have a much higher bar for deciding who is on the winning side of everyday life in this country. In fact, telling the audience that their community of faith was on the winning side - in a city where what side you're from can often affect whether you end up on the winning side of life - is a powerful affirmation.

So then the question becomes: What is the winning side? For the speaker, the winning side was wherever God was present.

*"The blessing of God comes with the presence of God,
when God's presence is treated the right way.
The presence of God does not show up
in places with slick technology,
it appears where people are willing
to humbly and powerfully worship
...to acknowledge God's worth-ship."*

The speaker has introduced the idea that God's blessing over our lives depends on us *doing* something. That it is not automatic. That it is not the default setting of having money, or living in a nice neighborhood, or being born as a citizen of a powerful country. He is contending that we have to be in God's presence in order to experience God's blessing.

In a cultural moment where there seem to be an infinite number of life paths to arrive at *#blessed* status, the speaker's words challenge us to think about whose blessing we have and whose blessing we seek.

The speaker pushed this line of thinking a step further when he offered this thought:

"Anger and fear will keep you from the presence of God."

All sorts of people want to blessed, regardless of their perspective on matters related to the divine. For those of us in communities of faith, saying *"God bless you"* at a gathering is as common as people saying *"How are you?"* at the office break room. For those of us who live in the United States, hearing a politician conclude a speech with, *"And may God bless the United States of America"* is as common as people saying, *"Have a good one"* at the conclusion of everyday interactions.

But if the blessing of God is connected to being in the presence of God, and anger and fear keep us from being in the presence of God, what does that mean for so many of us in this moment?

As soon as we step out of our safe spaces and comfort zones, and begin to engage the other humans who live in our area and in our country; most of us have to use all of our strength just to hold back our anger at - and fear of - those "other" people.

- What if God is not with you in your anger and fear?
- What if my anger & fear is keeping me from the blessing of God?
- What if we can't have it all - anger/fear - and the blessing of God?

PRACTICAL
{AUSTIN & LAKE}

This morning, I approached Chicago's west side by taking a drive down Lake Street through the suburbs that lie just three miles from the city's border street of Austin Blvd.

You can understand a lot about the history of Chicago over the past 50 years by taking a ride down Lake Street. From the gas stations and fast food restaurants in Maywood, through the tree canopied streets of River Forest, through the urbanized suburban bustle of Oak Park, and into the two-flats, corner stores, and 19th century mansions of the Austin neighborhood on the city's west side.

To ride down Lake Street into the city is to see the clear boundary lines between struggle and success, poverty and profit, comfort and carnage. Even the viaducts and walls of the Green Line tracks that run alongside Lake Street reflect the stark shift in the economic realities at the city's Austin Blvd. border.

◊

This building has the feeling of a meeting hall. With the exception of the stained glass windows along the side walls, there are not any immediately visible decorations that indicate what this space is used for.

There are around 150 people here, but it doesn't feel like it. It feels cozier, and more intimate. On the front stage, a small group of singers leads the audience in a series of songs. I was struck by the force of their performance. If you only heard them, you would think that their sound was coming from a larger group on a larger stage.

This Sunday happens to be Youth Sunday, and a 20-person team of young mime actors and praise dancers from elementary to middle school age have filled the front stage and main center aisle.

This team appeared to be comprised of about 75% young girls, and they performed their choreographed role playing and dance routines to an upbeat song with the chorus: *"He brought me this far, he will take me all the way."*

There is a specific kind of joy and freedom that is expressed when children dance. In some ways, this kind of joy can only be expressed by children. As I watched their performance, and the enthusiastic support of the adults in this building, I wondered what it means in the lives of these young people to have started their week in this way. I thought about the drastically different Sunday mornings their neighborhood friends and classmates must be having. What does it mean for these young people to have such a space to dance, sing, perform, play, and express?

◊

As the speaker approached the podium on the front stage, he encouraged the audience to *"go ahead and check-in on Facebook and Instagram, to let people know where you are."*

This was definitely a shift from the usual start of such moments, where the instructions usually involve reminders about silencing phones, not taking video of the event, etc.

The subject of the speaker's talk was: *Helping the Next Generation Win*. This talk was so practical, immediately applicable, and relevant to this moment.

He shared a powerful framework for parenting:

"As a parent, grandparent, re-parent...it is our responsibility to direct and dedicate our children so that we narrow the paths they go on."

I found these parallel tracks of direction and dedication to be a practical guide for all people engaged in the work of raising and developing young people. For the speaker, providing direction meant *"narrowing bad choices"*, and dedication meant *"giving back to God what he has given to us."*

*"The goal of parenting is to leave a legacy.
And that revolves around two questions:
(1) Have we prepared our children for life on their own &
(2) Did we prepare them to be fully functioning adults?"*

The idea that the purpose of parenting is to direct and dedicate children, and that the test for successful parenting is whether the children become fully functioning adults, is both inspiring and sobering. It's so clear and practical that it immediately helps parents assess what they're doing with their kids...but it also gives a clear and practical way for the parents to judge what was done with them when they were children.

I wonder how many of the parents assembled in this hall have had a chance to deal with (and work through) the psychological, social, emotional, mental, and spiritual consequences of how they were raised?

- Are we only able to raise prepared and fully functioning children if we were raised by prepared and fully functioning adults?
- And even if you were raised by prepared and fully functioning adults, is that enough to raise children, if the neighborhood you reside in is not prepared or fully functioning?

BEAUTIFUL
{95TH & EGGLESTON}

An uptempo jazz/afrobeat instrumental plays through the auditorium speakers as I enter. The front stage is wide and low, close to the level of the seats on the main level of the auditorium. In the middle of the stage, there's a ship steering wheel with a face that appears etched on it.

Although I was seated two rows underneath the balcony overhang, and approximately five rows from the back of the main level, I did not feel far from the music and presenters on the stage.

As the event was about to get underway, a woman walked up to a podium at the side of the front stage:

> *"In keeping with our African tradition, may we have permission to proceed with our worship? To signify, wave your handkerchief."*

With that, a procession of choir singers entered the auditorium, accompanied by the syncopated beats of African drum players on the front stage. Nearly every choir member was wearing a West African-inspired dashiki, dress, head wrap, or kufi.

In the first 15 minutes, the people assembled in this space experienced a wider and more global expression of love for God than most people will see in a year. The opening song was performed with a reggae vibe. The opening meditation was offered in Spanish and English. The opening prayer was delivered in Jamaican Patois. The mime/dance performance that followed was set to a gospel ballad.

The time set aside for the audience to greet the people seated around them lasted for a good five minutes, one of the more joyful breaks of this kind that I've seen so far. The band played a jazz instrumental while people embraced, laughed, and smiled at each other.

Another speaker came to the podium on the front stage, and began reading the names of people who had requested prayer, along with the names of those who had recovered from an accident or illness. As I have seen in other places during this journey, the overwhelming share of the prayer requests were related to health challenges and upcoming medical procedures. I was reminded once again that the frailty of the human body - and the mortality of the human life - are the great equalizers of human existence.

In keeping with the Afrocentric theme of this event, the main speaker began his talk by quoting a Langston Hughes poem, and said to the audience:

> *"Langston Hughes offers to us what the world*
> *claims to not be true - that you are beautiful.*
> *Real beauty forces us to pause and ask if we've encountered*
> *a human who has come in contact with the divine."*

This presented a series of interesting questions for me. First, the timeless question of: *What is beauty?* In this case, instead of the discussion around what is beautiful devolving into an argument about facial symmetry, body types, sexual attraction, and the power of American media; the speaker challenges us to recenter our notions of who we find beautiful towards those who have encountered God.

Second, how do we know - or how can we tell - when a person has encountered God? The speaker made a powerful point during his talk that I think gets at this question:

> *"God is always using the people who have experienced brutality to*
> *bring beauty into the world."*

How we respond to such a claim reveals something about our perspective on God's nature. How many of us, when asked to display or produce something beautiful, begin looking for something that has been brutalized?

The most creative, visionary, and artistic among us are able to reflect and mimic God's approach to beauty whenever they take the rough and raw materials of life and transform them into something the rest of us can appreciate as beauty.

The speaker challenged the audience to be among those creating beauty in the world:

"You beautify other people by using words that let them know that they are a child of God."

A person cannot give what they do not have. So we cannot hope to give and create beauty in the world if we have not identified it within ourselves. This goes far deeper than your level of self-esteem or self-love, both of which can exist without actually seeing yourself as beautiful.

It is this essential and difficult work - the work of seeing yourself as beautiful despite the brutality you may have experienced or witnessed - that I reflected on as I thought about the speaker's closing words:

"You cannot wait for other people to validate you.
It is your divine responsibility to validate what God put in you.
I am beautiful because of the simple idea: God made me."

NOURISHED
{WASHINGTON & PARKSIDE}

This stretch of Washington Boulevard is lined with 3-story brick flats and large apartment buildings. As I crossed the street, I came upon a swooping, concave building with a wall of tinted glass windows. Arrows chalked on the sidewalk directed visitors to the double-door entrance.

I followed the small flight of steps towards the faint sound of a piano two floors above. As I walked through the hallways and into the auditorium, at least five people shook my hand and greeted me with a smile. Two of the greeters introduced themselves by name, and asked me for my name. Another greeter explained to me that the events usually take place in their gym, however, due to a recent flood in the gym, they were temporarily relocating to the space I was entering.

And an impressive space it was. It was the library which serves the high school that is run by this organization. This library had a loft layout: high ceilings, modern light fixtures, and an exterior wall with floor-to-ceiling windows that opened to a sunny courtyard containing a small playground for children.

On the wall across from the windows, college banners hung over the loft railings. Chairs had been arranged to face the exposed brick wall at the far end of the library. Along the short, open staircase which connected the main left to the loft level, a paper banner with the phrase "I MATTER" was affixed to the brick wall. Next to the staircase on the main level, a piano, drum set, electric keyboard, and short podium formed the main stage.

◊

As the event got underway, 10 minutes were set aside for audience members to meet and greet each other. Many people got up and out of their seats, and walked throughout this room greeting each other.

Later on, a group of people visiting from Nebraska were recognized by a speaker at the front stage. The speaker mentioned an initiative called The Compassion Experience, which was some sort of intercultural exchange program with the goal of spending a day in the life of someone from a different culture. In fact, during my visit, there have been multiple references to events that involved promoting reconciliation and understanding between people from different races. This is the first time so far in my journey when racial reconciliation was explicitly stated as an organization's goal.

A few minutes later, one of the organization's staff members was formally recognized for his promotion to a more senior leadership role. During this brief ceremonial interlude, older people gave short speeches affirming, praising, supporting, and encouraging this young man and his wife for their dedication to their marriage, to raising their children, and to their service to the organization. The elderly lady who was stepping down from this position also gave a short speech that passed both the title and the torch to this young man.

Then came the time for the young man to speak. I was moved by a particular portion of his acceptance speech:

"Why don't young people go to church? It's because of us. Forgive us for being arrogant Christians. I thank God for opening my eyes. I hope that we can open their eyes."

I was reminded in that moment of the essential need for mentors. A group of older people had taken four to five years to train this young man for this moment. And when it came time for him to step up, these same older people were there to affirm him in the fullness of his humanity, not simply on the basis of his usefulness to their cause.

I wonder how many young adults in the surrounding blocks are receiving this level of intentional nurturing and development.

Shortly after the young man's acceptance speech, the main speaker announced that the time had come for the children under 12 years old to head over to a different room. A small collection of children assembled in the center aisle, and the main speaker greeted them and prayed for them.

As I watched, I thought about the next 10-15 years of these young people's lives. I thought about what it will mean to them to have spent their childhoods in a place where a room full of adults - most of whom they knew personally - prayed for them nearly every week. I thought about their classmates and neighborhood friends. How many of those kids had *any* adult pray for them this week...this month...this year...or ever?

The main speaker moved into his talk, which referenced a line of text in the Bible which draws an analogy between a tree planted next to water, and a person who is connected to God through consistent and daily meditation on God's words.

The speaker spent some time discussing the role a tree's roots play in the life and health of the tree, and he made an observation that stuck with me:

"Roots are finding water sources that you can't see."

I think this thought really breaks down what a life of faith is about. First, it's about recognizing that there are some things that we need in order to live, some things we need in order to survive, things we need in order to grow, and things we need in order to produce. What are the things you need in order to have a full life?

Second, the main speaker is contending that some element of our being is tasked with finding these life sources, these things that we need. Trees have roots. What do you have to find the life sources you need? What does it mean if the thing we need to live, and the part of ourselves that is searching for that thing, exist at a level *below* the surface, beyond what we can experience with our five senses?

LONGSUFFERING
{114TH & CORLISS}

After taking the 111th Street exit off the southbound side of the Bishop Ford Expressway, I notice the large Area 2 Chicago Police Department building - which takes up multiple blocks - on my left. On my right, there's an industrial-sized vacant lot with a sign in front. The sign features an architect's rendering of a new Whole Foods distribution facility.

I turn onto Cottage Grove and drive past murals and street placards which commemorate the rich and proud history of the Pullman company for which this neighborhood is named. I pass by a mural of Harriet Tubman painted on the wall of a boarded-up corner store, which sits at the foot of the viaduct that carries the Metra South Shore train lines overhead.

As I turn onto to Corliss Ave. and approach my destination, it feels like I am entering the parking lot of a football stadium or an amusement park. Traffic cones form lanes that guide cars into sections of this massive parking lot, where all the vehicles seemed to be parked facing this impressive structure.

Inside, there were tables with Black History Month displays in the lobby. Three-digit seating section numbers were painted above the stadium-like entrances to the auditorium. A choir was on stage singing as I made my way to a seat a few rows into the lower mezzanine level.

This place is the size of a small college sports arena, but the people around me look comfortable. Many of them stood in their seats and joined the choir in song before the event began.

◊

About halfway through the event, the main speaker came to the podium and announced the title of his talk:

"What are you doing in Gethsemane?"

Gethsemane is the name of a garden, and the site of a number of events that are central to the Easter story in the Bible. In a moment of rhetorical honesty that I won't soon forget, the main speaker opened his remarks with the following statement:

*"I couldn't prophe-lie to you,
I don't believe in pimping God's people."*

For the speaker, the garden of Gethsemane was a serious place, where serious suffering took place, and as such, warranted serious talk. In stating that he was not here to *"prophe-lie",* he challenged the audience to critically examine the other times they had heard other speakers make promises and proclamations about how soon times of serious suffering were going to end.

Rarely in my life have I been in a spiritually-oriented space and heard a speaker begin a talk by acknowledging the limits of their words. In the faith tradition practiced by the people assembled in this space, it is common to hear speakers make bold declarations about what will happen, where it will happen, when it will happen, why it will happen, and how it will happen. It is also common for audiences to reward such speech with respect and admiration for the speaker's confidence and clarity.

But today, this speaker did the opposite. He drew an analogy between the Garden of Gethsemane, and the times and places in our individual lives that press on us and/or crush us.

Referring to our personal gethsemanes, the speaker told the audience, *"I don't know when you'll get out,"* but that we can either view these periods of life hardship as *"gardens of grief"* or *"gardens of growth".*

He offered some useful tips for what to do when we find ourselves in a Gethsemane moment, and we're waiting for the time when we can exit from a place of suffering:

- *Engage in isolation. There are times when you need to be by yourself.*
- *Connect with your crew - people who will pray for you and not prey on you.*
- *Prayer will either change your situation, or it will change you in the midst of your situation.*
- *Pray that God's will is done in [your] life. He will give you the power to accomplish His will.*

His fifth and final tip stood out the most to me, because it was so counter-intuitive:

"What sense does it make to rush God through the process he is taking me? I've had times when I pressed the accelerator when God was pulling the parking brake."

I found this to be useful on multiple levels. The idea of not rushing God is something most of us struggle with. Do you ever wish you could speed through the Gethsemane moments of life, and park when times are good?

In saying that God is *taking* us through a process, the speaker introduces the concept that, sometimes, the events in our lives occur because God *intended* for them to happen. This raises the age-old question:

- If there is a God, why would bad things happen? Or at least, why would bad things happen to good/innocent people?

What I found helpful and clever about the speaker's framing was not so much that our process may include some very sad and painful Gethsemane moments, but that God is taking us through them.

In order to take us, God has to be present. Before we enter. While we're going through it. At the end. Throughout the aftermath.

So if God is taking us through anything, there are guaranteed to be at least two parties present in whatever you have to endure: You, and God.

LOVE
{KEDZIE & ALBANY}

On this morning in Logan Square, the main boulevard is busy with joggers, parents pushing strollers, and double-parked cars in front of two large Catholic churches.

As I walk up to my destination, I notice the massive Roman columns buttressed against the brick walls on the outside of this building. Inside, the auditorium is comfortable. Rows of recessed lights overhead, rows of long, cushioned benches on the floor.

An upbeat gospel song plays softly over the loudspeakers as people enter the auditorium in groups of 2-4. Everyone seems like they have known each other for a while. They are comfortable with each other, and are in the middle of extended conversations as the event begins.

A six-person band led the audience in a song with the chorus, "*A mighty fortress is our God*" as the main speaker came to the front stage and offered this commentary to the audience.

"Back then, 400 years ago, when the [song's] author wrote these lyrics, a town or village without a mighty fortress was in big trouble. And today, without a strong fortress, you and I are in big trouble."

The band then led the audience in another song, and about 10 people formed a line along the base of the stage and invited audience members to come forward if they wanted someone to pray with them.

As some people in the audience walked up to the front stage, one or two members of this 10-person team prayed with them. Some of these prayer sessions lasted for several minutes, yet the members of the 10-person team seemed okay with taking the time, no one seemed to be in a rush.

I watched as each person who walked up to the front concluded their prayer session by raising their head, smiling at their prayer partners, and embracing them in a heartfelt hug.

I was moved by watching similar scenes unfold at the front stage, for what seemed like 10 minutes. I wonder what it must have meant to the audience members who participated to begin their week this way.

I was reminded of the times when I've seen people in parks, malls, and busy streets holding signs that say *FREE HUGS*. We know that so many people in our country suffered from a lack of love and touch before the isolating effects of the coronavirus pandemic. People who may have been skeptical about the importance of non-sexual, love-filled touch are now increasingly on board with the idea.

- What could happen if more people found places and spaces where they could get a prayer and a hug?
- What could happen if more people found places and spaces where they were free to unburden themselves and share their concerns with someone who was willing to listen and not judge?

Later, the speaker made his way back to the podium on the front stage, and began his talk with the following analogy:

"You are without excuse if you came here and did not believe, or were unaware, that somebody was here before you. Although you don't understand who they are, where they came from, or how they got here...somebody laid this carpet, built and placed these seats, and laid the bricks that built this edifice.

Likewise, you understand that all you see was designed by a creator. A rose petal is not the result of an explosion somewhere."

The centuries-old conversation around the relationship between science and faith is a conversation for another book. What was interesting to me about the speaker's analogy was trying to imagine what our response would be to someone who walked around this building, entered this auditorium, and was unconvinced that forethought and planning had gone into this space.

The speaker's point seemed to be directed towards those in the audience who were okay with the idea that there is a force or entity, which is larger than themselves and existed before they did, playing some role in the world they see around them. Then the speaker asked a question that raised the tension between this force and us:

"How does God respond to our ignoring, neglect,
and rebellion towards him?
God responds with outrageous love...with love that
does not believe it will prevail in every heart;
but love that does believe it can win in any situation.

The love of God is outrageous in part because
he is loving people who don't love him,
and though this love will not win over every heart...
God's outrageous love brings and gives all of itself...
sacrificing His best,
and persisting in the face of rejection."

It is this understanding of love that I find helpful in trying to understand who God is.

- If the purest form of love is 100% bringing, and giving, and persisting, how many people do I truly love?
- How many people do you love at this level?
- How many of us have received that level of love?

TIMELESS
{37TH & WENTWORTH}

I first noticed this building while by on the Dan Ryan Expressway a month earlier. Surrounded by the White Sox baseball stadium, a high school, housing projects, and an eight-lane super highway; it feels like this building is a monument to a south side that existed decades ago.

So when I walked into the building, having arrived early for the event, and took a seat in one of the padded benches toward the back of the auditorium; I was not surprised to see the crowd seated around me made up mostly of senior citizens who were concluding their early morning Bible study session.

They ended their session by singing a hymn a cappella. They all seemed to know the hymn's lyrics, and they sang those lyrics with the kind of soul that only comes from having lived for many decades.

As the seniors gathered their things and began their procession out of the auditorium, I felt like I was watching some sort of *Benjamin Button*-like time lapse video. Leaving the auditorium were the steady, slow steps of the elders in their two-piece suits and long dresses. Entering the auditorium were the confident and steady strides of the millennials, rocking manicured beards, shredded jeans, and pencil skirts.

A 20-person group of singers entered the front stage and led the audience through a medley of hymns that were being remixed by the four-man band playing on the right side of the stage. In the middle of this joyful and energetic medley, a speaker walked up to the center podium.

"To properly enjoy this experience, grab four people next to you and ask them what God has done for them."

And for the next three to five minutes, the audience turned to each other and smiled, and hugged, and shared.

◊

A few minutes later, the main speaker approached the podium on the main stage and began his talk. He told a story from his childhood, a story about his grandmother's cooking and his mother's ability to stretch the leftovers from his grandmother's meals. The speaker told the audience that when - as a child - he would express disappointment that a meal was going to be made from leftovers, he said that his mother told him: *"These leftovers are in the hands of a master."*

The speaker then connected this story to his larger point:

> **"You've never made a better investment than putting your <u>life</u> in the hands of the master. God doesn't need anything to work with. God can do more with less than we can do with more."**

I thought this was a useful statement, because it highlights one of the fundamental questions we each must answer when thinking about how we understand God.

- Do you think of God as the force that set up all of the universe like a massive set of dominoes, pushed the first domino, and is simply watching how it all plays out?
- Do you think of God as a referee, calling fouls when humans make mistakes, and ejecting them from the game of life when they've committed one too many offenses?
- Do you think of God as a detached authority figure like your boss or the police, who you try to avoid by staying out of trouble or by not getting caught?
- Is God more like a father-figure, uncle, or coach, who made you do a bunch of stuff you didn't want to do when you were young, but who's kinda cool now that you're grown up?

So many discussions around God, faith, and spirituality are rooted in how an individual frames their understanding of who or what God is. For the speaker, at least for the purposes of this event,

God is way-maker, a guide along the uncertain and perilous path of life.

> *"God uses uncomfortable circumstances to develop unwavering trust as He works out His intended purposes."*

I thought the speaker's most powerful point came while he was talking about a story from the Bible about a boy, some bread and fish, and a big crowd.

> *"The disciples were looking to feed the people a little,*
> *while God was waiting to feed the people abundantly.*
> *And in the school of sanctification,*
> *you will always have to take a course*
> *in faith mathematics.*
> *You take care of the addition*
> *and God will take care of the multiplication.*
> *The thing about the disciples*
> *is that what they lacked in faith,*
> *they made up for in obedience…*
> *and obedience is God's love language."*

The idea that God has a love language reflects the speaker's presentation of who God is. The speaker was not just encouraging the audience to trust and obey God. The speaker was making the case that God is *not* merely observing us to see whether we demonstrate our faith through obedience, but that God *cares* whether we demonstrate our faith through obedience.

The speaker's use of the phrase "love language" is a rhetorical nod to the best-selling book *The Five Love Languages* by Gary Chapman, which was written to help people understand how others receive love.

For the speaker, God is capable of receiving love from humans, when humans demonstrate our trust in God through obedience.

Maybe that's what brought those seniors to Bible study early this morning.

RECOVERY
{GRAND & HAMLIN}

Nestled between several car repair shops, two-story brick flats, and some industrial-looking buildings is a low-key and relatively quiet set of blocks in the middle of the west side. So as I walked up the ramp that led to the front door of my destination, I wasn't expecting what I saw next.

I stood inside the open and sun-lit lobby and looked to my left. There was a small internet cafe with three computer monitors on a skinny table against the far wall, a few small tables, and a coffee barista booth. To my right, through the opened double doors, was a freshly-painted basketball half-court with a fiberglass backboard rim.

I continued forward into the auditorium as a gospel song played through the speakers. A skylight in the center of the auditorium allowed sunlight to pour in and soften the concrete floor.

As a band of seven people walked on to the long front stage, and as more people began to enter the auditorium, I was greeted at my seat by three people.

◊

Later on, the speaker asked the audience if anyone had any noteworthy events that the group could pray about or celebrate. And for the next five minutes, the speaker listened to announcements of birthdays, upcoming overseas vacations, family gatherings, and the deaths of close family members.

The speaker seemed to know many of the audience members - young and old - by name. I haven't seen anything quite like it on my journey so far.

20-25 children between kindergarten and eighth grade then assembled along the front stage like they were going to sing in a school play. The speaker led the audience in a prayer for them before they were escorted to another part of the building for activities designed for their age group.

This place seems to be centered on the needs of children, and their parents. The children looked very comfortable and very free in this space. I thought about what having a place outside the home or school where they felt safe would mean for them as they headed toward their teenage years.

◊

The main speaker approached the podium on the front stage and began her talk with an excerpt from the writings of a 14th century author named Julian of Norwich, and asked the audience to repeat the author's words in unison:

"All shall be well,
And all manner of thing shall be well."

The speaker's talk was less of a speech, and more of a series of reflections about dealing with sadness and recovering from emotional pain. Her calm tone reflected years of life experience, and her soft voice mirrored that of a trusted aunt, a therapist, or a yoga instructor.

She offered several thoughts that I found to be beautiful expressions of the relationship between the mental and spiritual aspects of life. Her points built around an often-referenced quote in the Bible: *"Not my will, but Yours be done[1]."*

She then offered this candid and sober thought:

"We can't fix the world. Our focus should be on doing our part in service....We're here for a short season to do what God has prepared for us...and we might not see the sun come out in our lifetimes."

That last sentence stopped me in my tracks. It's the kind of idea that is rare within the context of modern American life. The notion that God has put each of us here for a purpose, and that we may not even live long enough to see things around us get better, challenges each of us to consider whether our understanding of God requires this kind of present-day selflessness.

---

[1] Luke 22:42

The speaker was holding the very real darkness present in the behavior of some humans up against the very real understanding of God having a plan for each human. This tension is at the heart of one of the oldest questions about God:

- If God exists, why do so many bad things happen in the world?

For some people, it is the knowledge of darkness in the world - whether within ourselves or within others - that can lead to depression.

The speaker bridged the seemingly impossible gaps between her "all will be well" introduction, her pragmatic "we can't change the world" interlude, and her belief that each of us has God-directed work to do during our time on the Earth:

> *"You find yourself when you give yourself away...*
> *It's about releasing and letting go.*
> *If you ever think about taking your life*
> *switch to giving it.*
> *Don't swing with your emotion,*
> *stay steady with your devotion.*
> *Take it one day at a time.*
> *Keep going."*

CLARITY
{78TH & RACINE}

My drive into the city began in the grassy meadows and blooming trees of the county forest preserves that envelope the southwest suburbs, through the strip malls and well-maintained lawns along this section of the city's border.

The streets were quiet as I rolled into the Auburn-Gresham neighborhood on this sunny, spring morning: A few not-yet-opened soul food restaurants, a few gas stations, a few posters for a upcoming rap concert hanging from a few traffic light poles.

The sound of bells rang out over the neighborhood from a tower high above the street as I walked up the block towards this massive cathedral. This building reminded me of villages in western Europe where the cathedral is the largest structure in the village, and was constructed at an impressive scale to both inspire awe and reverence for how big God is, and to remind humans how small we are in comparison.

A large stone staircase at the side entrance led me into the main hall - an open space with tall, vaulted arches that held up the ceiling about 75-100 feet above my head. Dimly-lit chandeliers hung from the arches. Sunlight shining through the stained glass windows balanced the dark wood paneling along the base of the walls.

A rectangular table on the center stage is covered in Kente cloth, with three lit candles resting on top. Behind the stage hung a large painting of a Black man with a short afro, extended arms, and opened hands. Hanging from the ceiling, a neon sign with the letters: J-E-S-U-S.

◊

This 8:30am session audience is predominantly made up of senior citizens, and the cushioned benches are about halfway filled as the event begins. After some announcements, an older gentleman wearing a suit and bow tie approached the podium on the center stage and offered this thought to the audience:

"If you walked in here today, you are blessed.
If you can hear me today, you are blessed."

As the older gentleman concluded his remarks, an eight-person band came to the center stage and began to perform an uptempo gospel song. Along the wall to my right, a small procession of people circled the front section of wood benches in the hall, and formed a line on the center stage and joined the band in song. The first man in the procession was wearing a robe and holding a wood-

CLARITY {78TH & RACINE}

en cross. Walking behind him were a young woman also wearing a robe, another person who was holding a large hardcover book, and a middle-aged man wearing a robe.

◊

A few minutes later, the middle-aged man approached the podium, he was this early morning session's main speaker. What followed were two parallel situations, one of which I was prepared for, and one that threw me off completely.

First, the speaker was presenting an interesting talk about what it means to be a disciple.

> *"You can't simply call yourself a disciple*
> *simply because you're here on Sundays.*
> *A disciple is a worshipper.*
> *A worshipper is not someone who talks to impress people.*
> *A worshipper is true in their spirit.*
> *They are not faking it.*
> *A worshipper is someone who is in tune with God,*
> *and who talks to God."*

So there I was, on one hand sitting and thinking about where I stood on the disciple-worshipper spectrum, and on the other hand I was sitting and thinking about the large elephant in this large room: I could not hear the speaker clearly.

I heard the sound of his voice, but something about his microphone, the acoustics of this hall, or the location of my seat near the wall resulting in me only making out every third sentence he spoke.

This was the first time anything like this has happened on my journey. Naturally, I looked around at the other people seated around me, most of whom were senior citizens. *Were they having trouble hearing this talk too?* I couldn't tell. Most of them continued to look at the speaker with the diligent focus of an attentive student.

I wonder if the speaker knew that someone was having trouble hearing him clearly. I cannot have been the first person to have this experience. But I didn't say anything. I sat there, straining to hear, struggling to understand.

What happens when it's hard to hear God? What do you do when you tried to listen? You showed up, you strained your ears, but you only seem to be able to catch pieces of what God is saying to you?

What happens when you look around and it looks like everyone else is hearing God just fine? How do you say, *"I can't understand you, God?"*

I let these questions run freely through my mind as I tuned out of the rest of the speaker's talk. As the event came to an end, the audience stood and joined hands while reciting an often-referenced prayer from the Bible.

A few minutes later, the band performed a mid-tempo chorus with the following lyrics:

"So you get up and stand up
God has more than you can imagine
There is more God has for you
Faithful and true
He came so that you can be free"

The band played through this chorus several times, and I was moved by how those words spoke to me so clearly when just a few minutes earlier I had been in frustrated confusion.

Maybe when you can't hear God clearly,
or you can't understand what God is saying to you,
maybe the key
is to stay.
Stay open.
Stay attentive.
Stay,
and don't leave
or tune out.
Just stay.

EVERYWHERE
{ROOSEVELT & TRIPP}

Taking the Independence Blvd. exit off the Eisenhower Expressway leads me south down a well-paved, tree-lined stretch of road that connects two of the largest parks on the city's west side - Douglass Park and Garfield Park. One right turn changes the scenery to the alternating vacant lots and strip malls along this stretch of Roosevelt Road.

I pull up to the large structure which occupies an entire city block. The far side of this building is bordered by a mix of new and old two and three story brick flats on a quiet side street. Across the street, an industrial-sized lot lies vacant. My destination is easily the nicest building in this area.

I walked through the recently-paved parking lot towards the entrance, which was not like anything I've seen so far on my journey. The entrance was canopied by an extension of the building's roof, which gave the entrance the feel of a front porch. The small exterior stairs leading up to the front door were covered by clean, short , gray carpet; and were held down by evenly-spaced railings.

◊

Three older women in long dresses joked with each other at the front door. The lobby had the feel of a banquet hall, and lead directly to the auditorium.

As I found a seat on one of the padded benches a few rows from the back and looked around, it was clear that the designers of this placed had been inspired by the phrase *God's House*. From the vaulted ceilings of the A-frame structure, to the beautifully crafted stained glass windows where the people in the depicted scenes had a soft brown color used for their skin. On the wall high above the front stage, and the 25-person black-and-white robed choir, rested the words: *Serving God through Serving Humanity*.

As the event began, a speaker came to the podium on the front stage and asked the audience to join him in repeating the following declaration three times:

"God loves you too much to leave you where you are."

Later on in the event, 10 minutes were set aside for the collection of donations from the audience. Like a graduation ceremony procession, row-by-row the audience walked up to the front stage and placed their donations in baskets. It was a beautiful display of the people from different walks of life who make community in this space. There is something powerfully uniting about seeing so many people participate in this public act of giving.

Afterwards, the audience spent around five minutes hugging each other and exchanging *"God Bless You"* greetings. The people here seem to genuinely know each other. I could hear it in the audience's acknowledgement of all the people who had birthdays during this month. I could hear it in the request of the main speaker for everyone to get the word out about the upcoming annual celebration of those who had graduated during the spring, from any level of schooling.

◊

Then the main speaker came to the podium on the front stage to give his talk. He shared one thought that stood out to me:

> *"Any place on Earth where mortals exist,*
> *you are in God's territory.*
> *God is close by.*
> *Is there any place on Earth*
> *where God is not close by?*
> *So you don't have to send God anywhere."*

We are in a moment when nations and their borders are a major topic in the news. But humans have been drawing borders, defending borders, and going to war to expand borders for all of recorded history.

From the halfway line drawn between two siblings forced to share a bedroom, to the property lines drawn between homeowners co-existing on a section of land, we spend a lot of time and energy declaring what space is ours.

However, this underlying premise of much of our daily interactions is challenged by the speaker's idea that all spaces humans inhabit are God's territory. For the speaker, this idea is rooted in an understanding of God as the creator of all that exists, including this planet we call Earth.

- How does this view of God impact our understanding of who we are on Earth? Are we each tenants with a lease as long as our lifetime? Are we property managers whose job is to maintain that which we do not own?
- Secondly, the speaker's idea introduces a parallel question to the *"Why am I here?"* question of life. Now, we are being asked to consider: *"Why is this planet here?"*

The last line of the speaker's thought - that God does need to be sent anywhere because the whole Earth is God's territory - is also a usefully provocative statement that helps to illuminate our core beliefs about who or what God is.

For some people, the idea that God does not need to be sent anywhere is profoundly comforting. For them, this means that there is no place, hardship, or danger that could happen where God is not present to aid, comfort, and heal.

For others, the idea that God does not need to be sent anywhere is deeply troubling. For them, this means that the tragedies and hardships being experienced by people all over the world occur while God is present. This leaves them fearful and unconfident that God's presence is sufficient to prevent suffering.

What do you think?

TEMPTATION
{23RD & MICHIGAN}

This section of the city borders neighborhoods with histories and legacies that reflect the parallel universes which exist in this city. To the west are the Dearborn Homes housing projects. To the north are the restaurants, condos, and offices of the rapidly expanding South Loop. To the south, the historic cultural mecca of Black Chicago life - Bronzeville. To the east are the hotels and convention centers of McCormick Place.

This space blends in perfectly with the newly constructed condominiums and office spaces. A sandwich board sign has been placed at the corner of the sidewalk intersection to direct people towards the entrance.

The heavy black curtains covering up the storefront windows facing the street, and the soft lighting coming from the high ceilings, give this space the feel of an art gallery showing or VIP album release party. Inside, several people greet me as they setup video projectors and microphone cables. There are four small square tables with chairs in the back of this meeting space, and two sections of hotel conference room-type chairs neatly arranged to face the small front stage.

I could faintly hear the voices of a group practicing a song in a room nearby. There were only a handful of people when I arrived, but everyone seemed to know each other. People chatted in small groups of 2-3 while the band members set up their equipment on the front stage.

◊

A few minutes later, three women joined the band on stage and began to lead the audience in song. Although there were only around 30 people in the audience, the three singers sang with a level of passion and energy that was inspiring. You would've thought the audience was 10 or 20 times as big. I was moved by their dedication to excellence in their gift.

◊

A little while later, the main speaker came to the podium on the front stage and began his talk. He referenced a story in the Bible involving a powerful man who made a highly immoral decision and compounded it with a series of lies and cover-ups.

The speaker used this story to talk about situations when we are not being our best selves. Times when we choose to settle and compromise our values, morals, and standards. Times when we choose to take the low road.

> *"The opportunity to engage in foolishness always presents itself when you're somewhere you're not supposed to be. Whenever you have moments of great victory, you are more susceptible to great temptation."*

And then - in what might be the first such moment during my journey - the speaker mentioned the devil (aka "Satan"). A new book could be written every year for the rest of time covering the innumerable ways that humans think and talk about God's archnemesis.

The way we think about who or what the devil is (or whether we believe such a entity/energy exists at all) is inextricably linked to how we think about who or what God is.

- Is the devil simply the mascot for evil, with a pitchfork and red body suit cheerleading for Team Negativity?
- Is the devil the CEO of Hell, Inc., providing leadership for Hell's supernatural employees/minions to release darkness and mayhem in the world?
- Is the devil better understood as the founder of the religion of Evil, someone who died a long time ago, but whose ideas still live on through the current followers of the belief system?

For the speaker, the devil is the spiritual being that lives to oppose both God in heaven and the light of God within each of us.

> *"We talk about the devil stealing our stuff.*
> *The devil don't want your stuff,*
> *he is not intimidated by you winning,*
> *he wants to destroy your witness.*
> *When people find out about your moral failures,*
> *it negates your witness."*

Earlier, I intentionally avoided using any gendered pronouns in reference to the devil. In the quote above, the speaker introduces the pronoun *he* to describe the devil, consistent with how many faith traditions personify the devil as a man.

Which leads me to wonder how much of our personal understanding of God as being male, female (or both) affects our view of the devil.

- If we think of God as male, does that automatically make the devil male?
- Does the same apply if we think of God as female, or as having both male and female characteristics?

The questions are endless, but let's return to the speaker's talk; because it was his prescription for how to respond to moments of temptation and moral failure that I found powerful.

"You wanting to do right doesn't mean you're going to do right. Most people fail because their spiritual side is not strong enough. You have to put your spirit man in the gym."

I like this idea of your spirit being a muscle, and it needing to be strengthened like every other muscle in our body. I like this framing because it complicates our understanding of moments when we have to make tough decisions. Moments when we could do something that goes against the beliefs we claim to hold. Moments when our values and our identities are tested. Moments when we are tempted to walk in darkness.

Muscles are strengthened and maintained through a delicate blend of tension, resistance, stretching, exertion, and rest. Too much of any one of these, and the muscle can be damaged or weakened.

The tough thing is that we wake up each day and enter the world with less than full control over how much our spirits will be exercised. And if we're being honest, we have almost no control over the things that happen to us or any ability to space out life's challenges so that we can rest our spirits when we need to.

So every day of life is a spiritual workout. Some of us may have the ability to rest and take a break more than others, but you never know when your period of rest will end and the workout of temptation will start again.

AWAKE
{GARFIELD & PAULINA}

Driving down 55th Street from the west, I pass through blocks that alternate between the urban bustle of small business districts, and the residential quiet of stretches of single-story brick bungalows. This scene eventually gives way to Garfield Blvd. - one of Chicago's Grand Boulevards - with its grassy, tree-lined median and blocks of brick two-flats and greystones.

If this stretch of road was 5500 North instead of 5500 South, it would be a tourist destination. Rents and home values would be through the roof. In fact, this is the case in Hyde Park, the neighborhood surrounding The University of Chicago, where Garfield Blvd. terminates. But further back west, by Ashland Avenue, Garfield Blvd. simply serves as the northern border of Englewood.

As I walked up to the brick structure, an elderly woman was taping a flyer for an upcoming community event on the front door. I said good morning and she asked me how I was doing. I said I was well, and I returned the question.

"Blessed, as long as we keep fighting evil with good," she responded.

Inside, a handful of people were scattered around the main hall. A few elderly people, a few children. Behind my seat, two teenage boys were setting up the sound board as a gospel song began to play over the hall's speakers.

There were two sections of chairs arranged into seven rows facing the front stage. The main hall has the wooden paneled, A-frame vaulted ceiling of a small cabin in the countryside. The center of each wall contained a series of yellow and blue stained glass windows.

As the setup continued, a lady walked up to me and shook my hand:

"Are you our visitor for the day?"
"Yes ma'am"
"Good."

A few minutes later, another woman came and introduced herself and welcomed me to this space. A few more minutes passed, a few more gospel songs played over the speakers. A gentleman walked over to me, shook my hand, and introduced himself. Then another man walked up, wearing a linen short sleeve shirt and holding a wireless microphone. He shook my hand, asked me for my name, and introduced himself.

Halfway into the event, there was a period of 10 minutes set aside for the audience members to greet each other. The six-person band played an uptempo beat as the 60-70 people assembled greeted, hugged, and laughed with each other. I have to say, I have been personally greeted by more people here than at any other place so far on this journey. This group truly embodies the word *community*.

◊

Shortly after, the main speaker came to the front stage. He was the same gentleman in the linen shirt with the microphone who had introduced himself earlier.

He began his talk by referencing an often-used phrase in our current culture:

"We're in a time when news travels fast.
Because of that, it becomes easy to find yourself lulled to sleep by
the modern conveniences you use on a daily basis.
This phrase has become one that we can say
and know exactly what it means:
Stay Woke.

It's easier to fall asleep, the more comfortable you are.
The reason we seek comfort is because we want sleep.
God says: Because you love comfort so much, Beware! Keep Alert!
Because when you fall asleep, that could be the time."

It's relevant to note that the speaker had made prior references to an excerpt from the Bible that states that no human will know the time when God will return to Earth.

This could lead to an interesting discussion about how our understanding of God is not only impacted by how we perceive God's level of daily engagement in the day-to-day affairs of human life, but also by how much our understanding is also impacted by whether we believe that God is so engaged in human life on Earth that one day God will appear in a physical, visible way on this planet.

That is a conversation for another day. Right now, I'm interested in another way to think about the speaker's statement. We could think about his statement as reminding us that our unique set of skills and talents could be called on - by God - at any moment. The speaker channeled this line of think later in his talk:

> *"It will help you to stay woke if you realize*
> *that what you do everyday is not for you.*
> *I know we were told, 'What God has for me is for me.'*
> *Sorry to mess up your favorite song,*
> *but what God has for you is for everybody.*
> *And so the reason I'm telling you to stay woke*
> *is because so many people are asleep.*
> *And how can we wake people...if we're asleep?"*

FIRE
{WABASH & ERIE}

It's a warm and sunny summer morning as I board the train headed into the city. I walked by the banks, coffee shops, and upscale clothing boutiques that sit at the base of the office towers which form city block canyons of glass and steel through the heart of the Loop. In less than 24 hours, these dormant streets will be teeming with Monday morning rush-hour life.

I pass by the occasional family or small group of tourists who are taking photos of the surrounding architecture and making their way to visit the skydeck at the Willis (Sears) Tower.

The pace picks up as I exit the 'L' into the River North section of downtown, which is comprised of the blocks that lie behind the city's famous Magnificent Mile stretch of Michigan Avenue. People are sitting outside of coffee shops, and packing luggage into the back of SUV taxis parked in hotel driveways.

The exterior of my destination looks like a library on an Ivy League campus, or the entrance to a large museum. A quick bit of online research revealed that this building was constructed nearly 100 years ago by a professional organization for surgeons, and was designed in the French renaissance style. Which makes sense. This is exactly the kind of structure one would imagine a group of doctors building one block west of the Mag Mile.

It is an impressive space. The dark, hardwood floors on the main level are flanked by theatre-style gallery seating areas along the sides, and a mezzanine overhead. The walls are decorated with ornate gold plated moldings and sculptures. Dark wood panels along the base of the walls give way to Roman columns and a large stained glass window at the center of the wall behind the main stage. Continuing up, the four walls form an octagon as they ascend to a large dome at the center, high above the floor where padded chairs have been arranged in two sections of seven rows.

◊

As I took my seat on the main level of the hall, I looked around at the young professionals, college students, and parents of young children assembled. The people here seemed not only to know each other, but to be at the same stage of life.

One person came over to me, shook my hand, introduced himself, and chatted with me for a bit. A few minutes later, someone else came over, greeted me, and introduced himself.

A nine-person band led the audience in a series of songs, then a few families came to the front stage with their young children to engage in a short ceremony where they publicly declared their commitment to raising their children with Godly values.

Then there were 5-10 minutes set aside for the audience to greet each other, and then the main speaker came to the podium on the front stage. He opened his talk with a sentence that I have not heard anywhere else on my journey so far:

"Try to think about the darkest day of your life."

Given the part of the city we were in, given the group of people who comprised the audience on this morning; a conversation about trying times, difficult circumstances, and trials and tribulations was the last topic I expected to hear addressed. So I felt like the speaker was in my head, listening to my thoughts, when he said:

"Don't be surprised when life takes a turn you did not expect. What can often happen is we think everyone else's life is shiny and all-together."

This, I think, is the main way that we get in the way of people who are trying to find God. The perception that people who claim to know God think they are perfect often leads people to conclude that God is like the owner of an exclusive club where the perfect are allowed to enter, the average are ignored, and the struggling are ridiculed.

I thought it was powerful that the speaker chose to frame his talk by speaking about the common and routine nature of the struggles of life.

> *"I'm glad difficulty is behind me, but more than likely, another trial will come...Your circumstances can change...Don't be surprised because trials are coming."*

The speaker's talk revolved around a story from the Bible where three young people from a community that had been recently invaded and overtaken stood up for their beliefs, opposed the ruler of the invading nation, and found themselves on the hot seat...literally.

By choosing this particular section of the Bible, in some ways the speaker is acknowledging that not all trouble is the same. Some bad things happen as 'Acts of God' - famines, floods, droughts, storms, earthquakes, etc. However, some bad things happen because you did what you thought was right. You stood up for your beliefs - particularly what you believed God wanted you to do - and someone in a position of power over you got upset.

Although the speaker did not articulate this perspective in his talk, I saw his words as a perfect way to engage so much of what is going on in our society in this moment.

> *"Half of our problem is that we don't expect the trial.*
> *The other half is that we take our eyes off of the one who can deliver."*

Here, as at other points during my journey, we hear someone contending for a view of God as actively concerned about (and engaged in) the lives of humans.

> *"Our faith has to be in God, and not in the outcome.*
> *When we make the outcome our focus, we make God an idol."*

A whole, separate book could be written about this quote. For many of us, how we understand God is directly connected to what we believe God has - or has not - done for us, for our loved ones, or for humans in general.

We all participate in this to some degree; whether by our disappointment in a prayer that has gone unanswered, or by our disappointment in human suffering that has continued unaddressed.

What does it mean to have faith in God and not in a desired outcome? I mean, don't we have faith in God to *do* something? Especially when we find ourselves in trouble that is created by opposing the ruling leaders of the societies we live in...aren't we exercising faith that God will intervene in what will otherwise be a deadly outcome for us?

All these questions ran around in my mind as the speaker continued. He then offered the following thought as a way to think about how God shows up in tough times:

"God does not save them from the fire.
He does not prevent them from going into the fire.
He saves them <u>in</u> the fire,
through the fire,
by going into the fire...
There is room in the fire for God."

LEVELS
{38TH & INDIANA}

One mile away from the Oakwood Beach and the shores of Lake Michigan, in the heart of the historic south side neighborhood of Bronzeville, sits a quiet set of streets directly four and a half miles south of the city's Magnificent Mile.

On this hot summer morning, I walk through a series of peaceful blocks populated by a scattered collection of stately greystones, older brick two-flats, and newly constructed townhomes. I walk past a beautiful, modern building that is home to a community service organization providing resources and assistance to youth who find themselves homeless.

A few minutes after I arrive in the sunlit lobby of my destination, I discover that the event times had been changed. I am one hour early. So I decided to walk the long way back to my car and planned to go get some coffee and wait.

To my pleasant surprise, there was a soul food restaurant open for a brunch just a block away. I took this unexpected detour and enjoyed a nice chicken and waffles breakfast, and made my way back to the event.

◊

Inside the main level of the large auditorium, stage lights hanging from the wood-paneled ceiling light up the rows of padded benches. Long vertical wooden slats form the wall behind the stage like a music recording studio. A TV camera hangs from the end of a large crane-like mechanical arm that extends from the bottom of the right corner of the front stage.

On stage, a team of eight singers leads the audience in song, accompanied by a full band and a 30-member choir decked out in white and brown robes.

◊

A little over half an hour later, the main speaker approached the podium at the center of the front stage. He began with this thought:

"There are levels and phases in all of our lives. I believe any time you reach any level or go through any phase, there will be a testing of your faith, a testing of your life, a testing of your spirit...to see if you are ready for the next level or phase of your life."

Here, the speaker is reflecting an understanding of God as our spiritual trainer, our faith life coach. In this framework, God is aware of all the events that will happen to each of us in the future, including the events that will be challenging for us to handle.

For the speaker, God does not intervene to stop these uncomfortable moments from occurring to us so that we can evaluate our level of progress by our response to these unwelcome events.

With this approach, the speaker presents God's relationship to us like the one between a parent and a child. God knows that some challenges we must confront in order to grow, that preventing challenging circumstances from entering our lives would stunt our growth as spiritual beings.

The speaker continued to work out this idea, using storms as a metaphor for challenging periods in life:

"There are certain storms you are used to.
But when an unfamiliar storm appears, you panic.
In order to go to the next level,
you've got to deal with your problems.
Don't patch them up,
don't smooth them over...repair it.
Deal with it...and leave it alone."

This idea - that challenging times are opportunities to not only see what spiritual level we have reached, but that they are also opportunities to confront our weaknesses and mend our wounds - is something we don't hear often in 21st century American presentations about God.

For many of us, our natural response to tough times is to go into survival mode. To shut down and shut out. Especially when the challenge is one that we have not confronted before.

The speaker is challenging us to be open in the face of uncertainty, and to commit to doing the work of identifying and addressing the issues that our personal life storms have exposed.

As with physical training, spiritual training is both about maintaining and strengthening what you already have, and about preparing to take on new exercises.

> *"When you go to the next phase,*
> *when you've come through your test,*
> *you're able to confront some things*
> *that you've never seen before."*

This is useful, because the reality of the human experience is that we pass through a series of developmental levels where we learn new skills, acquire new information, and solve new problems. Each time we achieve, a new set of challenges awaits us.

The speaker's words offer us an opportunity to see God giving us what we need to get through the challenges we face today, and preparing us for the challenges to come tomorrow.

ANCESTRY
{CLARK & LASALLE}

It is a hot and humid mid-July morning as I walk east through the neighborhood of Lincoln Park. The main streets are home to clothing boutiques and specialty pastry shops. The quiet, tree-lined side streets are populated with brick townhomes.

The neighborhood ends at the entrance of Lincoln Park, the 1,200-acre expanse along the northern section of the city's 26 miles of lakefront parkland. At this intersection, the city skyline appears like a picturesque mountain range behind the massive brick structure which is my destination.

◊

Several sets of dark wood double doors with carved moldings line the street-level entrance. Inside, I can hear the hum of voices as I walk through the chandelier-lit side corridor which wraps around the main auditorium. The corridor's stately brick arches open into a cavernous hall.

On the main level of this large hall, there are four sections of pull-down wooden seats that reminds me of a school auditorium. Overhead, the tiled stone ceiling reminds me of an old European cathedral.

A copper-plated railing marks the balcony that wraps around the oval-shaped auditorium. The balcony seats rise towards the sets of stained glass windows that have filtered the incoming sunlight into an array of yellow, blue, and green.

As the event began, a seven-person band led the audience in song. Behind them, tall and shiny brass organ pipes rose up along the auditorium's wall and were framed on both sides by large projection screens displaying the songs' lyrics.

◊

The main speaker came to the podium and began his talk by reading several lines from the beginning section of the second half of the Bible (which is referred to as "The New Testament" by people of Christian faith). This section begins with a series of names in a genealogy which begins with Abraham - the founding patriarch of Judaism - and concludes with the book's first explicit introduction of the story of Jesus.

The speaker then offered the following framework as a way to understand the importance of these lines:

> *"[These lines are] about someone (Jesus),*
> *written by someone (Matthew),*
> *to someone (the first century Jewish people)."*

I found this sentence to be the most important moment of the speaker's entire talk, because it raises several of the key fault lines that separate the way people think about who or what God is.

The first fault line is the idea that talking about God also includes talking about some*one* - the person of Jesus. For the purposes of this book, I'm not focused on attempting to cover the wide range of beliefs regarding who Jesus was or was not. I'm more interested in the more basic question of how we think about God on the spirit-human spectrum.

- Is God simply a force like gravity, which would never exist in the form of a human body?
- Is God a ghost-like spirit, invisible to our human eyes, but having some form we would recognize like a body?
- Is God particle-like matter - the core essence of all things, present in all forms of living entities on Earth?
- Is God like a really big human sitting in heaven, as is often depicted in media?

For some people, the idea that God would emerge on the Earth in the form of a "normal" human is obvious. For others, it's silly. For some, it's crazy talk. How do you see it?

Second, the speaker's explanation that the aforementioned lines of genealogy were written by someone - the disciple Matthew - also provokes questions that have a significant impact on how we think about God.

The idea that God emerged on Earth in human form, did human stuff and God stuff, and had followers who wrote about these words and actions based on the oral history passed down from eyewitnesses is central to the understanding of God in the Christian tradition.

But how much you trust that these first century humans wrote the stories down exactly as they happened has a huge impact on how you think about the Bible in particular, and sacred religious texts more broadly.

Furthermore, how much you trust all the other humans who have translated, copy-and-pasted, and reprinted these words during the past 20 centuries also impacts how you think about God.

It's one thing to believe in God.

It's another to believe in the people who wrote the Bible.

◊

Lastly - and most seriously for this current moment - is the speaker's explanation that the lines of genealogy were written to a specific group of people - first century Jewish communities living under Roman Empire occupation.

The idea that the person tasked with writing down the story of Jesus approached it from the perspective of the ethnic group to which Jesus (and the author) belonged brings up yet more questions for us to wrestle with.

What does it mean to situate God, not only in a human body, but in a cultural body?

And by virtue of the world events occurring at that time, what does it mean to situate God within a political context?

How is our understanding of God affected by how (or if) we accept this context?

What does it mean that God is presented in human form among only one ethnic/cultural group of humans?

What does it mean to read the words of the Bible in the English language as citizens (or residents) of 21st century America?

How is the way we engage with this presentation of God influenced by our own cultural context in the world today?

CARE
{NORTH & RUTHERFORD}

It's another sunny Sunday morning in the city as I make my way down North Avenue, a peaceful drive at this time of day. I'm on the stretch of this normally busy street which forms the border of the far west side neighborhood of Galewood and the suburb of Oak Park.

Only a few sections of Chicago's borders transition as seamlessly between the city and one of its neighboring suburbs. If you cross North Avenue on any of the side streets in this neighborhood, you would not notice much difference between the well-maintained lawns, tree-lined streets, and brick single family homes of Galewood; and those of Oak Park. Even my destination, with its small stone chapel design, blends in nicely with the neighborhood; facing North Avenue from the Chicago side.

I walked through the open wooden double doors of the front entrance. A small group of people were chatting and catching up in the lobby as I walked by. An older man greeted me and introduced himself.

The inside of the main hall matched its countryside chapel exterior. Small yellow and blue stained glass windows filtered the sunlight shining in. In the back corner, colorful coffee mugs decorated the walls of a coffee stand. Two sections of padded chairs in the hall were flanked on the left side by the tables where people could sit with their coffee or tea, and where young children could sit to draw and color.

Wood panels built in an A-frame structure form the roof of this small and inviting space. A brick archway formed the backdrop for the front area where a few microphones, a drum set, and a piano seemed to be more than enough for the five-person band who led the audience in song. I looked around as the audience members joined in the singing. Although there were only a few dozen people assembled here, there was a mix of individuals who appeared to reflect the many walks of life represented in the areas surrounding this building.

◊

Later on in the event, the main speaker came to the front to begin his talk.

"How does God view us?"

I always appreciate when someone raises a foundational question like this. Before I can engage a conversation about faith communities, religious texts, institutions, traditions, and all that other stuff, I should answer the question: *How does God view us?*

My answer will reveal an aspect of how I understand who or what God is, and how I understand who or what I am. For me, the operative world is *us*. How does God view *us*?

Me and you
and your family
and my friends
and your neighbors
and my coworkers
and your racial or ethnic group
and the people who share my gender and sexual identification

To ask the question: *How does God view us?* is to place all these very different human beings in the same category:

Humans. Mortal beings. Finite entities. The creations.

And to place God in the opposite category:

Immortal Being. Infinite entity. The creator.

The speaker then offered the following statement as an answer:

"God is for us."

Just like our response to the question: *How does God view us?*, our response to this declaration also reveals much about how we think about God and how we think about ourselves.

This is an active, engaged, caring presentation of God. In order for God to be *for* anything, God would have to be "alive"...or conscious...or awake.

In order for God to be for *us*, God would have to be aware that we exist as humans on planet Earth.

To say God is for us is to say that not only is God aware of things in general, and aware of humans more specifically, but that God is also concerned about us and cares about the quality of our existence.

I hesitate over these words because saying *"God is for all humans"* is tricky. You and I can probably name a few humans who live only for themselves, and who are certainly not concerned about all humans. It makes us uncomfortable to deal with the notion that God would be concerned about all humans, including those we are not concerned about.

- What happens when God cares about people we don't care about?

Most of us are comfortable with God being "for me", and for people like me.

- How comfortable are you with a declaration that God is "for them", and for people like them?

A projection screen hung from the ceiling, beneath the brick archway, and above the speaker's head as he spoke. Towards the end of his talk, a slide appeared on the screen which was one of the most elegant and powerful images I have seen during my journey.

The slide looked like an ad for a Silicon Valley tech startup. The left third of the slide contained a soft pastel green background, with no words or images. The remaining two-thirds of the screen had a white background, and the speaker's earlier statement appeared in plain font across the top of the white space:

"God is for you."

If God had a branding and marketing team, they would have shared this screenshot all over social media. This slide remained over the speaker's head as he left the audience with a trio of thought-provoking questions:

"Why would this creator care about me?

What's that thing that makes you question whether God is on your side?

What's the thing that keeps you from seeing yourself as God sees you?"

AMBASSADOR
{WASHINGTON & ALBANY}

It's another warm, sunny summer day as I make my way through the west side. A few street signs indicate that one of the city's largest parks – Garfield Park – is a short bike ride ahead. I drive through the park, past a flock of geese cleaning themselves and resting near the park's lagoon.

The streets are quiet as I turn on to a one-way residential stretch of Washington Blvd. My destination sits at the corner, facing a mix of old and new three-story brick townhomes and greystones along Washington Boulevard and a vacant lot along Albany Avenue. I get out of my car and walk to the curb. A single, empty glass bottle lays on the grass.

Cars are parked in the grass-and-rock lot next to my destination. A group of senior citizens enter the building through a side door next to the large stone stairs at the front entrance. As I stood at the base of the stairs, I glanced to my right to see a pole tied to the trunk of a tree, holding a small fiberglass basketball backboard and rim.

I entered through the glass double doors into the inviting and well-appointed auditorium. Oak benches with blue padded cushions give the main floor the feel of a library. Light colored brick walls frame tall frosted windows, which filter the incoming sunlight.

The warm tone set by the recessed lights in the ceiling highlight the soft brown wooden panels that form the wall behind the front stage. Declarations like *Prince of Peace, King of Kings, God is With Us* appear on the banners hanging all around the auditorium.

◊

An eight-person, all-male band led the audience in song as the event began. I think this might be the first time I've seen an all-male band on my journey. There were only 100 or so people assembled here this morning, but they seemed comfortable being in this space, and being with each other.

After the singing, a few minutes were dedicated to recognizing audience members who were celebrating birthdays. The entire audience sang *Happy Birthday* to the handful of people scattered throughout who stood and soaked in the love.

The main speaker came to the podium on the front stage to recognize and celebrate a few women who had recently volunteered their time and energy in service to the people of faith in this community.

The speaker then took a few minutes to call out and recognize a young man who had recently won an oratory competition. The enthusiasm in the building as the elders in this audience turned with collective pride and applauded this young man was a beautiful moment. I wondered how many young men in the surrounding Garfield Park neighborhood had experienced this level of nurturing and encouragement.

The speaker began his talk with a simple yet powerful declaration:

"God has expectations for those who call him their father."

I could spend the rest of this book unpacking this one sentence. The critical and essential ideas presented here are:

(1) God is a being capable of having a relationship with humans, and

(2) This relationship – presented by the speaker in a parent-child framework – comes with expectations from God.

Many of us are used to presentations of God which state that God expects us to do certain things, or that God expects us to do things a certain way. These presentations are built on an understanding of God as The All-Powerful Creator who is always watching us, keeping a record of our actions, and is both willing and able to punish us.

What is interesting to me in the speaker's presentation, is that our relationship with God not only precedes God's expectations of us, our relationship is the foundation upon which God's expectations are built.

I find this idea to be very necessary in this moment. For much of the past generation in the United States, people who claim to have a relationship with God have been more known for their expectations of everyone else's behavior, than by God's expectation of their own.

So I was encouraged when the speaker expanded his initial statement:

"The Lord instructs us that our role is [to be] ambassadors...that our job is to make a difference in the lives of those we come in contact with."

The metaphor of being an ambassador is helpful, because any group of people communicates a message to the world in who they choose to send as an ambassador on their behalf.

When a group of people sends an ambassador, they are looking to communicate and engage. In order to communicate or engage, an ambassador has to have an in-depth knowledge about the group they are representing, the group they are going to meet, the history of the relationship between the groups, and the present realities that form the context of their engagement. Ambassadors have to watch, and listen, and learn, and understand. Before they talk.

We understand this if we're talking about sending ambassadors to groups of people from another nation, culture, religion, or race. But what happens when ambassadors are needed *within* the group you come from?

The speaker's words were a useful guide as he situated the ambassador work of his audience members to the neighborhood streets which surround this building:

"Start with your community.
Our community is in trauma – [a word that] comes
from the Greek word for wound.
When you take a look around, we are wounded.
The issue is that we've been down for so long,
we don't know how to get up.
We need a word of encouragement...
that you don't have to stay where you are."

There should be no question – after the events which have taken place in the U.S. and around the world over the past few years – that personal, family, and community trauma extends far beyond the borders of any neighborhood in Chicago.

The past few years have exposed trauma in all corners of our society. Truth is being revealed, masks are being removed, lies are being exposed. While we have different traumas that are attached to different consequences and different solutions; *that* we all have trauma is no longer a topic for debate.

So what are ambassadors to do in this moment, in their communities, in the face of trauma? The speaker offered this thought:

"The Gospel says: I see you. You are hungry, you are without,
you are thirsty, you came from a broken home,
but I see you.
We ought to use the gospel the same way it touched us.
They ought not leave the same way they came."

RUNNING
{CICERO & BELMONT}

Quiet side streets of neatly-kept bungalows and two-story brick flats surround this stretch of Cicero Avenue; one of Chicago's busiest, most industrial , and – on this morning – pothole ridden thoroughfares.

The front entrance of my destination was bustling with activity as I approached on this warm summer morning. Two mini-buses were parked by the curbside, having recently dropped off people for the event.

The four sets of fiberglass doors remind me of the entrance to a movie theater. A short set of steps leads me into a modern and lively foyer. As I look around, it seems like my initial hunch was right, this building must have been an old-school movie theater in its previous life.

I see two theater-like entrances, with signs *Ages 1-4* and *Grades K-5* above their respective doorways. To my right, a series of iPads rest on stands for people to register for upcoming events and/or make donations.

An alternative rock inspirational song is playing over the speakers in the main auditorium, which is a grand hall with high ceilings, sculpted wall moldings, and stage lights hanging from racks overhead. It looks like it was originally designed for theatre performances. Two hotel conference sized projection screens rest on the walls, framing the stage where 30-40 choir members have joined the five-person band, who have begun to lead the audience in song.

◊

Midway through the event, a speaker welcomed the audience, and shared a little bit about the history of this gathering. She concluded her remarks by saying, *"We pray, and God moves. That is our history."*

Later on the main speaker walked on to the stage, and began his talk with a powerful opening statement:

"Maybe you're here today and you're running from God.
It's no use running, because wherever you're going to go,
that's where God is going to be, because He loves you so much."

The phrase *"running from God"* is a common expression within certain faith traditions, and for good reason. How a person processes that phrase reveals quite a bit about who or what they think God is.

- What does it mean to run from God?
- Is it a literal movement away from a place or group of people?
- Is it a literal movement away from a set of beliefs or values?
- Of all the ways to leave, why run?
- Is there a difference between "drifting away from God", "walking away from God", and "running from God"?

We're used to asking the question *"Where is God?"* when things go wrong in life. Is it possible for God to reply, *"Where are you?"*

The speaker continued:

> *"Receiving God's love is accepting that*
> *He knows you and wants a relationship with you*
> *– the good, the bad, the ugly –*
> *He already knows.*
> *If you try to serve God*
> *and it's not based on a love of God,*
> *it becomes about rules and regulations."*

The speaker's statement raises another set of fascinating questions:

- Is receiving love from God the opposite of running from God?
- Can you receive love and run at the same time?
- Do you have to run back to God to receive love, or is it enough to simply stop running?

One of the other interesting themes underlying the speaker's statement is that serving God is the result of (or the response to) receiving God's love. This framework provokes self-reflection:

- How do I respond to love?
- How do I respond to God?
- Does God's love create a responsibility to serve?
- Does a desire to serve come from a love of God?

The speaker continued on the topic of service and our relationship to God:

> *"You'll never be able to serve God*
> *if you're pointing fingers at Him.*
> *Most people don't feel good about themselves...*
> *they don't talk about it,*
> *but they don't trust God*
> *because they blame God."*

I think most of us would agree that our views about God are in some way connected to our views about ourselves. So we're left with another simple but deeply probing set of questions:

- Can we feel good about God, without feeling good about ourselves?
- Is it possible to love God and hate yourself at the same time?
- Is it possible to hate God and still love yourself?

As always, I have more questions than answers. I have learned to live with my questions, and I don't have some wonderful all-encompassing answer to end with, so I'll just leave you with the speaker's closing thought:

> *"When you can praise God for making you,*
> *you can say:*
> *'I've had lots of hurts, and sorrows, and pain,*
> *but He's not finished yet."*

RESTART
{24TH & WABASH}

It's fitting that the last unofficial Sunday of Summer 2017 would be another warm, blue-skied day in Chicago. In the midst of a month which will be remembered for the deadly rains and floods in Texas and Louisiana; and the record-breaking heat in California, the weather in Chicago has been exceptional this summer.

I exit Lake Shore Drive and pass by the gleaming new Marriott hotel, the stately Hyatt hotel, and the massive McCormick Place convention center. I pull up to a quiet, semi-industrial stretch of Wabash Avenue. An 'L' train passes by on the elevated tracks a block away.

At this intersection, there's a brick warehouse with brick-filled windows. Alternate colored bricks along the window bays mark where the original windows once were.

The parking lot next to the brick warehouse is cordoned off by a chain link fence, which has the words *Pray for Peace* affixed to it. Small construction equipment and vehicles are parked in the parking lot across the street.

Standing proudly at this same intersection is my destination, a stone, cathedral-like structure. It seems to serve as a marker to a time way before this part of the city looked like it does today. Three bell towers form the street-facing corners of the building. A large set of vertical stained glass windows rest in the middle of the building's exterior facade.

Two older men are talking casually outside of the entrance as I approach. I passed them, entered, and waited near an usher; watching as a group of 11 people stood in a circle, holding hands and praying. Once they finished, the usher greeted me and handed me a visitor's welcome packet - a standard-sized white envelope containing a brochure, a pen, and some information about upcoming events.

The meeting hall reminds me of a school library. Four sections of padded chairs were separated by three rows of the building's support columns. These white columns rose to meet the newly varnished wooden beams which formed squares across the white ceiling.

Along the right wall, wood beams and panels frame the doors and windows of small offices. To the left, an American flag rests on a stand in the corner. Behind the front stage, a small banner announces that this organization was celebrating its 170th year anniversary.

From 1847 to 2017.

Think about that. This organization was founded just 10 years after Chicago was formally incorporated as a city. People have been assembling as members of this institution since before the Civil War, the bicycle, the radio, and airplanes. I wondered if our generation will be able to start any organization that will still exist in the year 2177.

◊

As the event began, a three-line declaration was displayed on the projection screen behind the front stage, which the audience proceeded to recite in unison:

> *"I am a spirit.*
> *Who has a soul.*
> *And I live in a body."*

For the next few minutes, I marinated on those words. I don't think I've ever heard this particular framework of human spirituality presented before. The concepts of the spirit and the soul are very familiar to members of many faith traditions. And after a generation of Oprah's TV shows and the mainstream acceptance of yoga and meditation, a broad cross-section of the country has had exposure to a presentation of human life as "human beings having a spiritual experience."

However, this declaration goes a bit deeper. It puts forth the notion that we are each spiritual beings, presenting the spirit as the part of us which does not die and is connected to the divine.

The next part is the mind-blowing idea:

- What does it mean for a spirit to have a soul?
- If the spirit and the soul are two different things, which one is activated when we're trying to communicate with God?
- Do we control both our spirit and our soul?
- Do we control either one of them?

I return from my head-tripping daydream and notice that the main speaker is at the podium on the front stage. The first line I caught was a powerful one:

"We start doing things as requirements to get us out of a crisis. Then we stop doing the thing that got us out of the crisis."

It is part of the human condition to perform in a highly focused and disciplined manner when we're in a heightened state of awareness. When we're facing a threat. This is as true in our relationships with each other as it is in our relationships with God.

> We make promises and commitments.
> We start out with enthusiasm.
> We get comfortable.
> We lose our enthusiasm.
> We get overconfident.
> We slack off on our promises and commitments.
> We let our guard down.
> We become vulnerable.
> Crisis strikes.
> We are shocked back into action.

The speaker addressed this condition:

*"We don't understand the tools God has given
for abundant life...
prayer is one of those tools...prayer is the reset button."*

He went on to use a story about his recent battles with a slow-performing computer as a metaphor. He talked about all the problems he had been having when his computer started running slowly His tech person advised him to restart the computer and explained all the benefits of routinely restarting a computer.

I thought this was an effective and useful metaphor for thinking about how we engage with God in a world as fast-paced and crazy as the one we live in. It is very easy to go through our day with all our mental, emotional, psychological, physical, and spiritual capacities running at full speed.

Prayer pauses the flow of new stimuli from the world around us. It helps us refocus on the core, essential truths about our lives. As we work through the stages of Reflection, Gratitude, Admission, and Petition; the parts of ourselves which connect to God are re-energized.

Sometimes we emerge with new solutions. Sometimes we emerge with new strength to engage the craziness in our lives. Hopefully we are at all times reminded of our place in the universe, and of God's.

LOST
{RACINE & ADAMS}

For a city known for its harsh winter weather, the reality of yet another pleasant day in the city is not lost on me, as the southern part of the U.S. braced for the wrath of yet another hurricane.

The West Loop is marked by quiet and clean streets, new and renovated 3-5 story condominiums, lofts and offices - most of them converted from the warehouses and fresh food markets that once dominated this part of the city. People are walking with their kids, or with their dogs. The scene looks like the architectural renderings you see for new real estate developments.

Colorful vertical banners mark the parking lots and guide the way to the building's front entrance. Two steps into the lobby, and the scene looked like the opening of an independent film screening, art exhibition, or album listening party. There was a bustling coffee stand where young professionals and college students were gathered and talking in small groups.

To my left, on an exposed brick wall hung four light bulb-filled letters that spelled the word L-O-V-E. Nearby, more people were congregated and socializing, waiting for the auditorium doors to be opened. What was clear in my first few minutes in this building, was that this space had been carefully and meticulously designed for this crowd. And the people assembled in here this morning looked like they knew they were in a space that had been designed particularly for who they were, what they liked, and how they lived.

As the seven-person band led the audience in song and the house lights were dimmed, gentle clouds began to stream from a fog machine behind the front stage. Overhead, track lighting and stage lighting complete the concert-like atmosphere. Two of the building's large rectangular pillars have small handwritten inscriptions all over them. From what I can see, most of the inscriptions are Bible verses and inspirational quotes.

◊

Later on, the main speaker began his talk with a sentiment that I had been hearing recently on my journey, but it never gets old to me, so I'll share it again:

"I don't know why you're here at 9:30 in the morning,
but it gives me the chance to tell you
that there is no distance you can run,
no depth you can go,
where God will stop chasing after you."

We've been engaging this thought for a few chapters now. These metaphors - of us running away from God, of us running back to God, or of God chasing after us - are useful for revealing our view about who or what God is.

- When you hear the words, *"God will not stop chasing after you"*, are you comforted or horrified?
- How does this scene play out in your imagination? Is God angry or irritated? Is God anxious or afraid? Is God smiling or laughing?

These may seem like odd questions, but what I find odd is that conversations, discussions, or debates about God rarely seem to acknowledge the wide range of humans' instinctual, often subconscious reactions to the idea of God. And it's even more rare to talk about how we developed these mental images in the first place.

The speaker went on to set up the premise of his talk by using another metaphor:

*"The heist happens when we lose who we are.
The identity theft goes on inside ourselves...
You and I are just as capable of losing who we are in God.
How do you lose you? There are areas where we've disowned parts
of ourselves, and given others the right to define who we are."*

Each of us have many identities which overlap, intersect, and interplay in different ways at different points in our lives. Which aspect of ourselves we focus on (or present to others) is related to many factors and circumstances beyond our control. We are all affected by the spaces and people around us.

Particularly in this current moment, it's harder to detach from the daily craziness. When it's not as easy to find, create, or maintain the personal space and time to do the kind of reflective introspection that's necessary to know if we have indeed outsourced control over parts of our identities.

- How do you know when you've lost yourself?
- How do you know when people or circumstances have begun to define you?

The speaker then made a series of statements which are worth considering:

*"Only God can give you your true identity.
My wife does not complete me or give me my true identity.
No relationship can complete you. No success can define you.
Your true identity is God-given.
Only you can give it away, or trade it to others
for acceptance, love, or a place in the world."*

DEATH
{JACKSON & LARAMIE}

As the calendar transitions us from summer to fall, it appears like Chicago did not get the memo. This morning, yet another sunny Sunday in the city, the high temperature is expected to rise into the mid-90s for the third day in a row.

In a week where hurricanes and earthquakes disrupted - and in numerous cases, ended - the lives of people from Mexico to Puerto Rico to the Virgin Islands; I find myself especially thankful for electricity, air conditioning, and running water.

There is more traffic than usual on the Eisenhower Expressway heading into the city this morning. I look into the horizon, and I can see a blimp hovering in the air to the right of the city's skyline, a sign that the Bears must be playing at Soldier Field today.

As I exit off the expressway onto Central Avenue, I see two men standing and talking by the side of the off ramp. They are not holding any signs, they are not even facing the cars stopped at the red light. Yet, it looks like if they had a cool indoor place to go, they would rather be there.

Across the street, in the median, another man paces slowly amidst the foam cups, plastic bags, and other litter scattered around the on-ramp to the expressway. I glance to my right, and see a whole pile of garbage dumped along the side of this exit.

How did this happen?
How long will it take the city to clean this?
Who dumps a house garbage bin worth of trash on the side
of the road after exiting the expressway?

These questions lingered in my mind as I made my way down Central through the Austin neighborhood on the city's west side. I arrived on a beautiful stretch of Jackson Boulevard populated by well-maintained lawns, brick two-flats with a late 1950s architectural design, and one-story bungalows.

What I did not know as I walked up the short set of concrete stairs towards the front entrance of my destination, was that just six weeks earlier, two men had been murdered by gunfire on these very same steps, at nearly the same time of day as I was ascending them on this morning.

I learned about this tragedy after my visit - and to be honest - I probably would not have come to this location if I would have known about this incident beforehand.

- What does that say about me?
- What does that say about God?
- Is the violent death of these two men on these steps a sign that God has left this place, and the people assembled here?
- Is my unwillingness to visit if I would have known a sign that God has left me?

I don't know. What I do know, is that this building was still open on the morning I visited. People were still assembling in this space. And they were well aware of what had taken place here six weeks ago. I don't feel qualified to describe what that says about their connection to God. I do feel humbled and grateful to be able to - in some way - bear witness to this community of people.

Inside the oak wood front entrance doors, a narrow hallway wraps around the main auditorium. The auditorium is a uniquely-shaped semi-octagon. Clear lines of sight in every direction. Vertical banners hang from the ceiling's wood rafters, one banner on each side of the octagon.

On the left side of the front stage, a band of four provides the musical soundscape for the day. Rows of padded benches follow the building's semi-octagon pattern, and a few people were seated in each of the rows when I took my seat.

Above the speaker's podium, a skylight opens the auditorium to the bright blue sky outside. Three elderly men began the event by leading the audience in a series of songs, spirituals, and prayers. The vibration in the voices of these men - which was matched by the other people assembled here - seemed to channel the voices of their ancestors. There's something about hearing people sing who have been talking to God for a long time.

Later on, the main speaker approached the podium on the front stage and began his talk by referring to a well-known chapter of the Bible known as Psalm 23. This chapter, with its opening line, *"The Lord is my shepherd. I shall not want"* is memorized and routinely recited by people in Christian faith traditions.

The speaker then set up the framework for his talk with a powerful, yet counter-intuitive statement:

> *"Despite its popularity, it is not applicable to everyone...*
> *everything hinges on the word 'my'.*
> *Unless he is my shepherd,*
> *the rest of the psalm does not belong to me."*

This framework (that the benefits of a connection to God depend on an individual relationship with God) is useful. It provokes a series of questions that reveal yet another aspect of our beliefs about who or what God is.

- Does God only help people with whom there is a strong connection?
- How long does a person have to be connected to God in order to receive help?
- Who confirms the existence or status of our individual connection to God?

So many questions, so little time. Midway through his talk, the speaker started to list the benefits of having God as our shepherd. He said the following, which I thought was powerful at the time, but became even more profound after I learned about the recent events that transpired here:

"If the Lord is your shepherd,
you can keep fear from overwhelming you...
There are a whole lot of things that scare,
especially in the city of Chicago,
where everybody has a gun. Even God's people.
People will have you crazy,
but when you live in God's unchanging hand,
you can be safer than the person
living in the biggest mansion in the suburbs
with the best security.
He gives you the ability to sleep,
regardless of the circumstances around you.
And that's comfortable."

WORDS
{HOLLYWOOD & GLENWOOD}

A small, but noticeable chill has returned to the breeze on this fall morning. The humidity has dropped, the leaves are dropping, but the sun remains. It is another beautiful day in Chicago.

A book about Chicago would be incomplete without a ride on Lake Shore Drive, the beautiful highway that traces the lakefront, taking you from the city's northernmost neighborhoods to those at its southern edge.

Lake Shore Drive is best experienced when there is lighter traffic, either at night with the city lights on one side and the dark abyss of the lake on the other, or in the morning, where the full life of the lake is on display.

The joggers and cyclists along the lakefront, the 40-mile per hour, easy riding pace of the traffic, the miles of parks and trees which run along the drive, and the breathtaking architecture of the city unfold as you go from the south to the north side.

I have taken the drive today all the way to the northern end of Lake Shore Drive, which deposits travelers into the neighborhood of Edgewater, just blocks from the lake. I drive through quiet, tree-lined blocks of spacious two and three story homes, and brick apartment buildings. It's the kind of setting that encourages you to go for a walk or a jog around the block.

I almost missed my destination, it blended in so well with the surrounding buildings. There were two entrances - one set of double doors on the side of the building, and at the top of a flight of stairs, a young woman held the door open at the front entrance. She greeted and welcomed me as I walked inside. The small auditorium was a cozy, intimate space, like the kind of place where you might come to watch an independent play.

◊

Young millennials and college students were deep in energetic conversation, clustered in pairs and small groups as I took my seat. They look comfortable, with each other, and in this space.

A piano sits sectioned off to the left of the small front stage, which is framed by an oak wooden arch, beautifully affixed to the white wall. The interplay between the oak on the chairs, window frames, and doors, the gray carpet & white walls, and the sunlight coming through the minimalist stained glass windows...this place feels like the common room of a private college dorm. I feel comfortable. Two other people walk up to me and introduce themselves.

Later on, the main speaker approached the podium on the front stage and opened his remarks with a series of bold and provocative questions:

> *"Do you actively see the Word of God*
> *as the most valuable thing in the world?*
> *What is your spiritual attitude towards God's word?*
> *And could that be indicative of your posture towards God?"*

Just like a book about Chicago is not complete without talking about Lake Shore Drive, a book about God is not complete without talking about God's words.

For the speaker, the phrases *Word of God* and *God's Word* refer to the compilation of writings assembled in the version of the Bible used by members of Protestant Christian faith traditions. Books have been written about the Bible - its history, its composition, its accuracy - for as long as humans have been able to make books. I won't pretend like my book can even scratch the surface of this subject.

Instead, I want to zoom out and ask some more fundamental questions that may help us uncover yet another aspect of our views or beliefs about who or what God is.

At the root of any conversation about a religious book or document (the *Word of God* for purposes of this chapter) is the idea that God communicates with humans. What do you think?

If you're okay with that idea, the next premise is that God communicates general messages, which are intended for all humans.

Many people, with many different beliefs about God, are familiar with the idea of God communicating specific messages to each of us on an individual basis. A lot of us are okay with communicating with God on our own, by (and for) ourselves. But the idea that *God's Word* (as used by the speaker) deals with a situation when God had something to say to a *group* of people.

Some people told others. Some wrote down what they had been told. Some translated what was written down into other languages. Some compiled these writings into books. Some transported these books to other regions of the world. And so on, until we arrive to this morning, with me sitting on the north side of Chicago, listening to this speaker.

- How do you think about all the steps between the people who originally claimed to have heard a message from God and you reading this page today?
- Do you think that whatever people received from God thousands of years and miles ago should be received by you and I as direct communication from God today?

It was clear on this morning, that the speaker receives the words compiled in the Bible as words from God, as words of direct and relevant communication to any person who reads them. After referencing a situation recounted in the Bible, he made the following observation:

> *"They stopped work because fear overwhelmed them.*
> *God's people had become spiritually complacent*
> *and culturally compliant.*
> *What stops this? The Word of God.*

The Word convicts, stirs, and restores God's people."

There's way more to unpack in that quote than we have time for in this format. But I think even at the most basic level, there is something profound for us to reflect on.

Words from God help us deal with moments when we've become complacent in our spiritual lives, and compliant with whatever the popular mood of the moment is in the society. Words from God help us deal with times when we've stopped doing our God-given work because we're afraid.

Those are words worth knowing.

FAMILY
{79TH & WABASH}

It had been raining for the past three days, and for a while it seemed like the streak of beautiful Sunday mornings was coming to an end. But the skies cleared, the sun returned, and the streak continues.

As I drove east down 79th Street that morning, I'm reminded of the wide range of neighborhoods connected by this street. It is well-known that Chicago is a city of neighborhoods. More specifically, Chicago is a city of intersections. It is not enough to say you live on Pulaski, or North Avenue, or 79th Street. The real question is: "Pulaski *and what?*", "North Avenue *and what?*", "79th Street *and what?*". So much - from your quality of life, to your opinion of the city - depends on where you intersect any of the city's main streets.

Crossing the Dan Ryan Expressway on 79th Street, I entered a section of the south side with wide side streets, brick bungalows and two-story homes with larger-than-average front lawns.

When I arrived at my destination, two well-dressed older gentlemen were standing by the building entrance, next to another elderly man who was in a wheelchair.

The front lobby is warm and inviting. I walked through the wood double doors into the auditorium, which looks like three connected country cabins. The high A-frame ceiling is constructed from oak wood beams. The side walls are made of a tan brick, the kind you often see in elementary school buildings.

About halfway to the front, in the middle of one of the rows of padded benches, a lady was standing and praying in front of a small group of people. I took a seat and looked around. Most people in the audience were older, and it was obvious that they know each other and are comfortable with each other.

I was greeted and welcomed by three people as others entered and took their seats. There were six 30-inch TV screens positioned along the sides of the auditorium. Behind the front stage, five rows of empty benches rose stadium-style towards a soft gold curtain draped across the wall.

A bright blue neon light lit up a stained-glass cross at the top of the wall behind the front stage. Along the sides of the auditorium, frosted glass windows filtered the incoming sunlight through an array of blues, greens, and tans.

Four singers joined an eight-person band and led the audience in song as the event began. A few minutes later, in what was a first during this journey, a speaker came to the podium on the front stage and asked all the visitors to stand.

So I stood, along with a handful of people scattered throughout the auditorium. The speaker welcomed us and thanked us for coming. She even offered to pray with us afterward. It was a unique experience to be welcomed so personally.

◊

Later on, a 17-year old high school student came to the podium and performed an a cappella song/spoken word tribute to her aunt, who raised her and brought her to this space every week throughout her childhood. The line in her piece that resonated deeply with me was when the young lady said:

"She loved God so much that it made me want to love God."

I thought of all the elderly women assembled here today, and how many children in the blocks surrounding this building had witnessed a deep and profound love for God expressed through their lives.

Afterward, another high school student - a young man in his senior year - performed a spoken word piece. Before his performance, the young man introduced himself to the audience.

He told us that he was on his school's wrestling team, that he also played football, and that he was member of the United States National Guard - to which he received an ovation from the audience.

He had arrived late this morning due to a health emergency with a member of his family. In that moment, I was again reminded of all the young people in the surrounding blocks, who are walking around with a combination of personal interests, unique threats, and family concerns. How many of them have a community of adults and elders stop to collectively celebrate their humanity, acknowledge their pain, and talk to God on their behalf?

◊

Finally, the main speaker came to the podium to begin his talk:

> *"I believe the family of faith is suffering*
> *from an ego mania in our culture...*
> *'How can I be better?'*
> *'What is my blessing going to look like?'"*

This is a common lament among people of faith, especially in the U.S. It is not that different than the concerns about the ego mania, narcissism, and lack of self-awareness that is regularly projected in popular media in our country.

What is interesting to me is the gap between the diagnosis offered by the speaker in that statement, and the diagnosis that would come from people who are not affiliated with a formal faith tradition.

I wonder what the response would be if we asked those outside the family of faith what we are suffering from in this moment. Do we even want to know?

- How do we think about the critiques of people who don't identify with our beliefs about God?

- Do their opinions matter?

- Do they matter as much as ours?

- Does it depend on whether they are talking about society in general or talking about us as a society (or family) of faith?

The speaker continued:

> ***"We are moved off course and purpose,***
> ***which is faith in God.***
> ***Every now and then it's time to get past ourselves,***
> ***the responsibility of every believer is to glorify him."***

One of the questions we could ask in response is: Why?
Why do we have to get past ourselves?
Why is it our responsibility to glorify God?

And I remember that line from the high school girl's poem:

"She loved God so much that it made me want to love God."

PERSONAL
{WASHINGTON & KILDARE}

The streak has ended. The weather report indicated that there was a chance of showers this morning, and that possibility has turned into a reality.

The rain begins to fall as I make my way north through the middle of the west side. Traveling through this section of the city can only be described as passing by block after block of what *used to be*. Those buildings *used to be* the headquarters of one of America's largest telephone manufacturing companies This building *used to be* a warehouse. That one *used to be* a factory.

As I turn on Madison Street, I passed a boarded-up, trash-filled, abandoned building; where campaign posters for a local politician hang ironically from a chain link fence

Even this majestic building which is my destination used to be something else - the center of life for a community of Irish Catholic Chicagoans who have long since migrated away from the surrounding neighborhood of West Garfield Park.

As I cross the intersection towards the massive stone cathedral edifice, two older women in ponchos were handing out flyers for an upcoming protest against a few prominent national politicians. I have the sense that these women were neither residents nor frequent visitors to this part of town.

◊

Your first impulse when entering this hall is to look up towards the ceiling, and along the walls. Two sets of large stained glass windows depicting what I assume are scenes from the Bible rest in the walls closest to me. In the middle of the hall, a pair of beautiful circular stained glass windows face each other from opposite sides of the hall. Beautifully restored murals cover the walls above the front stage. The faded brass columns along the walls are decorated with moldings, and build up to the impressive vaulted ceilings high overhead.

14 men led the audience in song, accompanied by a young, well-dressed man playing the organ, and another one playing the drums. Although many of the audience members were senior citizens, there was definitely a cross-section of people from the community assembled here.

This is such a traditionally religious space, inspired by a very different culture, by people who sung very different songs…and yet, the people here this morning are moving freely and comfortably in this space. They seem to be at home here. This ability to make home, in spaces designed by (and for) others, is a part of the history of faith we don't talk enough about.

Later on, five minutes were set aside for audience members to greet each other. A man in a suit greeted me, introduced himself, and invited me to an upcoming Saturday brunch where the men of the community gather.

As I was about the return to my seat, I noticed that no one was in the rows of benches around me. In fact, no one was in any of the benches. The audience members had made their way to one of the three main aisles in the hall and began to stand side-by-side, holding the hands of the people next to them.

Once everyone was standing, a young woman went to the front stage and began to pray for the entire crowd. She said a lot, but one line in her prayer stayed with me:

"Even through all this, thank you."

I looked around at all of the people standing. I wondered what each of them been through this year. I thought about what each of them had seen this year. I thought about what each of their families had seen and been through this year. Yet here they were, holding hands, demonstrating the calming and healing power of human touch. It was one of the most uplifting expressions of community I have witnessed all year.

Then the main speaker came to the podium on the front stage to give his talk. About halfway through his talk - which was referencing the writings of one of the Jewish prophets - the speaker started talking about what happens when God communicates specific messages to us as unique individuals.

> *"God gives him a vision.*
> *It's a vision that has not yet come to pass.*
> *God has to give you something to run with...*
> *you need your own vision...*
> *You need something where God is real in your own experience. You don't need a generic God, you need a personal God."*

There are quite a few interesting ideas raised by the speaker's words. First, he has added another dimension to our ongoing reflections about our perspective on who or what God is.

In our post-Enlightenment, post-modern, post-everything world of 21st century America, everything is personal and few things are universal. However, for many people, God still falls in that shrinking category of the general/universal.

- Can a general/universal God communicate custom-tailored messages to specific humans?

Ironically, many people still seem to agree with the idea that specific humans can communicate custom-tailored requests and messages *to* God.

We have many ways of describing the experience of receiving a custom-tailored message from God. Some people say God spoke to them, in a dream or in a quiet moment. Some people say God sent them a sign. Some people say God gave them a vision. Some people say God touched their heart or their spirit.

We humans spend a lot of time arguing about the God *out there*. What name to call God, what God looks like, what God's gender is, where God resides, who God likes, who God hates, and on & on.

But what about the God *in here*?

Different societies, in different regions of the world, at different points in history, have displayed a wide range of reactions to humans who express a desire to communicate with the God *in here*. In their minds, in their spirits, in their psyches, in their souls, in their essence. And whether these individuals were embraced, ignored, or rejected; they persisted in this quest to experience God on a personal level.

What does that say about God? What does that say about us?

GATEWAY
{KEDZIE & MONTROSE}

It's a beautiful, sunny, and cool fall morning as I make my way north on 1st Avenue, through the forest preserves which also form a nearly continuous border along the northwestern outskirts of the city. Fittingly, I turn east and enter a pleasant stretch of road called Forest Preserve Drive, which deposits me on to Irving Park Road on the north side of the city.

I pass by the strip malls, Catholic schools, and small businesses of Portage Park and Irving Park until I arrive in a section of quiet, tree-lined streets, filled with single family homes and brick two and three-flats.

I walk up to Kedzie, make a right turn towards my destination, and wind up on what must be one of the most diverse blocks in the city. To my left, a renovated three-story brick apartment building with a hair salon in its storefront. Next to it, a vacant lot is fenced off. Across the street, a small mom-and-pop Mexican restaurant sits next to a car repair shop, which sits next to a Walgreens.

In the distance, the sun reflects blindly off the bronze dome of a large building. A few blocks to the right, I can see the tops of cathedral-like spires rising from another large structure. My destination is on the other side of the vacant lot next to the hair salon ,a nondescript two-story brick office building.

◊

I'm running a few minutes late, so the sound of music was already coming from the auditorium as I walked through the fiberglass doors and up the stairwell to the second floor. An 11-person band was performing on the front stage in front of a large TV screen, flanked by a smaller screen on each side of the stage.

As I took my seat in one of the padded hotel conference room-like chairs, a video began to run on the large screen. It featured a young woman who appeared to be sitting in a TV news set, presenting information regarding the organization's upcoming events. I can't say I've seen anything quite like this on my journey. The video included a weather forecast, a comedic sketch routine, and a rotating globe graphic in the bottom corner of the screen!

Later on, a speaker came to the podium on the front stage and gave a presentation about the good work this organization was doing in the surrounding neighborhoods through their food pantry.

They had partnered with community members from the neighborhood to provide *"food people actually want."* The speaker formally recognized two community members who assisted with the food pantry and were in the audience this morning.

The speaker noted that this partnership - between members of two different immigrant groups residing in Albany Park - was doing such a good job of providing *"food for all"* that the neighborhood's alderman highlighted the work of the food pantry in the ward's monthly newsletter.

◊

As I joined the audience in applause, I felt a deep sense of pride. Although, it wasn't a sense of pride that came from accomplishment. I did not do any work related to this food pantry. I did not donate money or goods to this effort. I did not even know the pantry existed until five minutes ago.

My sense of pride did not come from a shared experience with the audience members assembled in this space. I did not know anyone here. I had not participated in the life of this community. I don't even live on this side of town.

And yet, the strong sense of pride that welled up within me came from a sense that these were *my* people, a sense shared by many Americans when they are surrounded by a critical mass of people whose ethnic ancestry traces back to the same country or region as their own.

The sense of pride is even stronger when that shared cultural identity is unfamiliar, disregarded, or demeaned in the eyes of the dominant culture.

Here were people who were from the same place my parents are from. People whose movements, language, and clothing emerged from the same region as my family's.

Here were these people, in this city, reflecting the image of God, in this way. It brought a smile to my face.

A book about Chicago would be incomplete without a mention of the city's historic legacy of playing a key role in the voluntary - and forced - migration patterns of ethnic groups from around the world. And the neighborhood of Albany Park has been an important part of the city's history. As one article I read explained: *"Throughout the 20th century, Albany Park acted as a gateway community for aspiring middle-class ethic groups.[1]"*

Gateway communities have been essential to the survival of newcomers throughout Chicago's history. Gateway communities hold up welcome signs when others say: *"Get Out!"*

Gateway communities help newcomers transition by starting with what is old and familiar as a foundation to learn about what is new and foreign.

Gateway communities treat newcomers as humans, not issues. A gateway community is a home base, a refuge, a safe space, a slice of home...a place from which you can begin again.

---

[1] "Albany Park." Encyclopedia of Chicago. Accessed August 22, 2018. *http://www.encyclopedia.chicagohistory.org/pages/36.html.*

For an individual who is a member of a cultural or ethnic minority in this city, gateway communities allow newcomers to see examples of people like them who are surviving and thriving in this new land.

Some neighborhoods and communities are gateways for people who are new to the city and/or country. However, some communities of people are also gateways for others who are newcomers to God.

◊

Later on in the event, the main speaker came to the podium to give his talk. There were several lines in his talk that challenged the audience to examine how we treat newcomers:

> *"How do you related to people who don't*
> *look, smell, or act like us?*
> *Immigrants who have arrived recently,*
> *we were once like them.*
> *At one time, I was shopping at the thrift store...*
> *it wasn't always like this.*
> *Are you sensitive enough to the needs of those around you?"*

"We were once like them." A powerful phrase made even more powerful by the implicit acknowledgement that *we* could be like *them* again.

The speaker continued:

> *"There are people who have better degrees than you,*
> *yet you're in a better situation.*
> *If not for the grace of God, where would you be?*
> *There is no way you will meet other people's needs,*
> *and God will not meet your need."*

It is that ability,
to see someone in their most vulnerable moment,
to identify with them,
to see yourself in them,
to see God in them,
which reveals God in you.

CHANGE
{CHICAGO & GREEN}

The streets are quiet and relatively empty as I make my way into the city early on this cloudy Sunday morning. It rained last night, and it feels like everyone just decided to pull up the covers and sleep in today.

My drive reveals a city on the move, under construction. I pass through the ever-expanding Medical Center district, from the new condos and lofts of the West Loop, to the converted warehouses and factories of the River West neighborhood. Old black water towers remain perched on the roofs of many of the surrounding buildings, a reminder of the 20th century industries that built this city.

Although different industries run the city now, and different groups of people live in this neighborhood; as I approach my destination – which is across the street from a concrete mixing facility and the Chicago Tribune newspaper printing warehouse – I am reminded that old Chicago is still here...at least for now.

◊

The first sign that I was in for a quality experience appeared in the middle of Chicago Avenue, in the crosswalk that led to my destination. There were two millennial-aged people serving as crossing guards, equipped with hand-held stop signs and pausing the traffic for the streams of people walking towards a building set back from the street.

I was warmly greeted by two more young people as I walked through the building's front door. The best way to describe my immediate impression is that it felt like I walked into a really dope underground silent party, film screening, or art show. This is a young and diverse crowd. The tables in the middle of the lobby remind me of the first week of college, where the campus is full of organizations promoting their work.

There is a small coffee stand next to the bustling lobby. Inside the auditorium, the aisle stairs lead you down through the tiers of stadium-style seating sections. The front stage is close to the seats, and is equipped with a fog machine that puffs gentle clouds into the air. An uptempo EDM/dance track is playing. The exposed brick walls finished off the building's impressive interior décor.

It is a cool November weekend morning, and there are 350-400 people packed into this intimate theater-like venue, and they are mostly younger. College students, 20 and 30-somethings...and they are very much present, engaged, and enthusiastic. This was an inclusive atmosphere with the cool aesthetic of an exclusive venue.

As the event began, the 12-person band on the stage began to perform a song with the chorus, "You Got Me." As they sang, stage lights beamed concert-like rays of light across the audience, and seven high-definition projection screens displayed the song lyrics overlaid on video clips of nature scenes and abstract light animations.

I looked around and thought about the capital and resources that must have gone into this space. It was so clearly and intentionally created for the audience assembled here. Faith communities are often portrayed in popular media as people operating in physical spaces created by earlier generations. Yet this space was clearly designed by and for this current generation.

◊

Then the main speaker walked onto the stage and began his talk with a bold rallying cry:

"It's time to turn the page.
One of my goals is to not recognize myself year after year.
The last thing I want to do is be known for who I've always been.
I don't want to get prayer for the same thing,
I want new problems to pray for."

The speaker's words raise a number of interesting questions that reveal another layer in how we think about who or what God is.

- How does our comfort level with change affect our comfort level with God?
- Is it possible to be connected to God if you're not comfortable with change?
- Is being highly comfortable with change the only way to be highly connected with God?

The speaker continued on the topic of change:

> *"Is anybody in here interested in changing the world?*
> *If you truly are, you'll be obsessively consumed*
> *with the Holy Spirit changing your life.*
> *Less fingers pointing at others to change,*
> *more thumbs pointing at yourself.*
> *If there is change in you, there will be change around you."*

A conversation about the meaning and use of the term Holy Spirit within the Christian faith tradition is centuries old, and is beyond the scope of this book. For the purposes of this chapter, it is enough to understand that the speaker is using "Holy Spirit" to refer to the element of God that activates the spirits of people through their encounters, experiences, and relationships with God.

For the speaker, a connection with God requires and results in a change in our lives. And that a change in our lives is the necessary prerequisite for seeing change in the world.

This is an interesting diversion from the messages the young people assembled here normally receive in graduation speeches, award show acceptance speeches, or motivational social media videos.

When we usually talk to young people, we tell them that they can be anything they want to be, and that, once they put their mind and effort to it, they can change the world.

But how do you feel about the concept that you can be anything God wants you to be, *after* God has changed you?

THANKS
{62ND & THROOP}

It is a beautiful, sunny, cool mid-November morning as I head to the south side. Some leaves are still on the trees, but it's the rustling sound of the leaves that have already fallen which is my favorite part of the season.

I drive down Garfield Boulevard, into a part of the city which has come to acquire a reputation for being dark and dangerous. On this morning the streets are peaceful, and bright with sunlight. A viaduct stands over the street a few blocks in the distance, underneath a few CTA 'L' trains parked on the tracks above.

A stray cat was hiding in the corner of the doorway entrance to my destination. Both of us were caught off guard by the other's sudden appearance, and after a five-minute staredown standoff, we decided that the other was not a threat, and peacefully went our separate ways.

A short flight of stairs opens into the auditorium. The red carpet on the center aisle divides the two sections of padded dark wood benches and hardwood floors. Sets of frosted stained glass windows shaped like baseball home plates line the walls. Dark wood chairs, podiums, and tables form the front stage.

This is a space that looks like it holds many stories and many histories. A glance at the front of the brochure I received when I entered stated:

Founded 1887 - Present Edifice Erected - 1923

I thought about the people who constructed this building, and who formed the first community that assembled in this space on a regular basis. This city was a very different place 94 years ago. I wondered what they hoped for this space, and for the streets that surround it.

◊

As the event began, a 10-person choir in white robes started to sing. They were mainly elderly folks, and although there were less than 20 people in the audience this morning, the choir members sang with enthusiasm, dedication, and joy.

THANKS {62ND & THROOP}

Why?

What are they experiencing in their spirits that enables them to still sing with such passion and conviction in the twilight years of their lives?

What have they come to understand about God?

About halfway through the event, time was set aside for audience members to pray. And then, nearly all of the now 40 people in the audience stood up and proceeded to the front stage; where they knelt side by side and began to pray silently, individually.

This was one of the most powerful demonstrations of solidarity and support I've seen all year. Each person, talking to God about their own concerns and challenges, pains and pressures; but doing so while kneeling alongside someone else who has come to talk to God about their own stuff.

It was a physical expression of their collective belief that God has both the capacity and the willingness to receive, process, and respond to all their different issues, at the same time, in a manner customized to the unique life reality of each person kneeling.

It was an admission of need,
of limitation.
An acknowledgement that they don't have it all together,
that they remain in need of daily guidance,
protection,
and assistance
from the Divine.

◊

After the audience had returned to their seats, the main speaker came to the center podium on the front stage. Her words so wonderfully captured the energy I was experiencing in this place.

I conclude this chapter with some of her words, for the times when you feel moved to kneel on the floor and communicate with God.

"When we realize how much we benefit from knowing God,
then we can fully express our thanks to God.
No matter how extreme our calamity,
God can break through to us.
Our God is a miracle worker, loving and kind
to those in distress...
The [West African Akan Twi] word 'sankofa'
teaches us that we must go to our roots...
to the best of what our past has taught us
[in order] to move forward.
It means to go back and fetch what we have forgotten.
Some of us have forgotten how to thank God."

REJOICE
{CERMAK & CANALPORT}

My drive down Archer Avenue this morning takes me past the mom-and-pop stores of Little Village, past McKinley Park, and into what initially seemed like a no man's land between Bridgeport, Chinatown, University Village, and Pilsen.

To my left, massive concrete caves form between the overpass beams of the Stevenson Expressway. To my right sit a mix of converted warehouses, banks, and single-family homes.

A lot is happening on the streets surrounding my destination. A beautiful mural brightens up the exterior wall of a small warehouse as two men tend to a community garden. Next to the street, trolley train tracks end abruptly at the building I am about to enter. A old train car has been permanently parked in the parking lot. It looks like it could be a breakfast-and-coffee spot, but I can't tell. There's an electric generator line running into it, so something cool is happening in there.

My destination is unique building, on a unique intersection, in a unique section of the city. It is a large four-story polygon structure, formed by a diagonal street, which makes the building appear larger. Its brick exterior is suddenly interrupted on one side by another building covered in black-and-white sketch illustrations. A new apartment/condo development has been built across the street. In the other direction, semi-trailer trucks sit quietly next to a power plant and a concrete mixing factory.

◊

I walk into the single door entrance, into a dimly lit loft like space. Murals and artistic illustrations line the exposed brick walls of the main staircase. A few neon signs shine patiently from the interior windows of a closed craft brewery bar.

For the first time in my journey, I almost got lost trying to get to the auditorium. However, there were people positioned at each landing of the main staircase to greet and guide visitors to the auditorium entrance. At each stairway landing, 8.5 x 11-inch paper signs pointed to galleries, maker workspaces, and artist studios.

"We're huggers here." The young lady standing at the entrance of the auditorium told me as I approached. True to her word, I was greeted with a friendly hug and cheerful welcome. In fact, I was greeted by at least a dozen people as I waited in my seat for the event to begin.

I was reminded that making strangers feel welcome in an unfamiliar space is both an art and a science. It requires strategic forethought and planning, yet can only be executed by humans who chose to engage others in a life-affirming and respectful manner. When a group of people do it well, the effect is powerful. I was glad I found my way here this morning.

◊

The auditorium's aesthetic reflected the artistic environment of this building and this block. A small rug and set of dark curtains formed the front stage where a two-man guitar band equipped with two microphones, two laptops, and two speakers provided the music for the event. The string lights hanging from the ceiling give this room the feel of an outdoor cafe.

Later on in the event, the main speaker walked in front of this audience of 30-40 people seated on padded folding chairs, and began his talk with a provocative thought:

> *"We get so excited about celebrating ourselves,*
> *other people,*
> *the next new thing,*
> *the next accomplishment.*
> *We don't want to rejoice,*
> *because God hasn't done enough for us."*

Rejoice is an interesting word, because it is a word that is not often used in daily conversation, at least not in the U.S. I cannot remember the last time I heard someone use the word *rejoice* outside of a faith community or religious setting. In fact, if you do a web search for *rejoice*, the top results are either dictionary definitions, or links to religious content.

Which is fascinating, because according to those dictionary links in the search results, the word *rejoice* means:

"to feel or show great joy or delight"
"to be full of joy"
"to be incredibly happy, or express your incredible happiness"

Think about that. We live in a country that has mastered the art of packaging and selling happiness to the whole world. Our entire way of life is built on the idea of striving for "Life, Liberty, and the Pursuit of Happiness". Yet we rarely use the word *rejoice* in our everyday lives.

- Why is that?
- Have you never felt great joy or delight?
- Have I never been incredibly happy?
- Is it that most of us do not feel great joy and delight often?
- Do we only express incredible happiness on certain occasions, in certain settings, around certain people?

- Do we rejoice about God?
- Do we rejoice because of God?
- Do we rejoice in spite of God?
- Do we rejoice independent of God?
- Does thinking about God produce great joy and delight?

For the speaker, there was a symbiotic relationship between rejoicing and gratitude. Later on his talk, he described this relationship beautifully:

> *"When you get alone with God...*
> *into the presence of God...*
> *allow thanks to overcome anxiety.*
> *Thanks opens the heart to rejoice,*
> *and rejoicing opens up a heart of thanks."*

TEARS
{79TH & COLES}

It is the first weekend in December, and it is gorgeous outside. Sunny, clear blue skies, temperatures in the mid-50s. Further confirmation that one of the stories of the year has been Chicago's run of great weather for much of it.

However, I see the weather report, and I know a cold front is coming in two days. So I figured this was a perfect day to take one more ride down Lake Shore Drive.

It was perfect. There was very light traffic as I passed McCormick Place onto South Lake Shore Drive. On the right side of the road, I noticed a newly-erected, simple square stone sculpture with the words *You Are Beautiful* engraved large enough for all passersby to read, even at 45-50 miles per hour.

As the lake gleamed in the sunlight to my left, I passed the Museum of Science and Industry, the Jackson Park marina, and the 63rd Street beach house. I continued on, past the stately brick three-story townhouses along Jeffrey Boulevard.

I arrived at 79th Street, and made a wrong turn; which ended up taking me past a beautiful 1920s-style theater house called The Regal. It's exterior - with one wall covered in murals honoring historical figures, and the other walls holding boarded windows below an aging marquee - was somber metaphor for the parallel realities of this part of the city.

As I turned around and headed east on 79th, the streets were quiet, the shops were closed, many stores were boarded up, and many buildings looked like it had been a while since a store operated there.

A short walk from the lakefront, the polygon-shaped brick structure which was my destination emerged on my left. A handful of people were scattered around this deceptively spacious auditorium when I walked in. On stage, six singers were running through their final rehearsals and sound checks.

The red carpet and red padding on the benches were offset by the building's cream-colored walls and the brass trim of the balcony railings. Since the building faces towards the lakefront and the auditorium's windows are close to the roof, the sunlight pours into this space, filling the auditorium with natural light.

◊

Midway through the event, the singers began a rendition of a song called *Total Praise* by Richard Smallwood. It is a song I have known for over 20 years, and it has been therapeutic for me at pivotal moments throughout my adult life.

So it was fitting that on this Sunday morning, one day after I attended a memorial service for a close friend, concluding a week of grieving and reflection, that I found myself tearing up as the singers sang the song's chorus:

"You are the source of my strength
You are the strength of my life
I lift my hands
In total praise to you.
Amen[1]*"*

As the choir ran through the series of melodic Amens in the song's bridge, I did not have it in me to lift my hands. I allowed tears to flow, and as the sun moved directly into the window over my head, I allowed myself to feel, and to heal. A few minutes later, an upbeat jazz saxophone solo completed my move from sadness to joy, in remembrance of my friend.

◊

A few minutes later, the main speaker came to the podium on the front stage to begin his talk. There must have been some other people going through their own sad times, because the speaker began his talk with a bold statement about the benefits of tough times:

---

[1]Copyright © 1990 Bridge Building Music (BMI) T. Autumn Music (BMI) (adm. atCapitolCMGPublishing.com) All rights reserved. Used by permission.

> *"When you're in a storm, you don't ever*
> *give in,*
> *give out,*
> *or give up.*
> *Blessings are always attached to burdens,*
> *and generally you go through burdens*
> *to get to the blessings."*

"Blessings are always attached to burdens." How do you hear this statement? Does it give you encouragement and hope? Does it leave you skeptical and unsure? Does it make you even more sad or angry?

How we think about God is as affected by the quality of our mental, emotional, and psychological condition as it is by our physical and financial health.

- Has the size of your blessings matched or exceeded the size of your burdens?
- Do burdens come into your life at the same speed and frequency as blessings?
- Do your blessings stay as your burdens come and go?
- Do your burdens seem to last longer than your blessings?

The speaker raised two additional questions that I found powerful for reflection and meditation:

> **"What do you do**
> **when you don't sense**
> **the presence of God**
> **in your storm?"**

> *"What are you dealing with*
> *that you've allowed*
> *to become bigger*
> *than God?"*

Many questions have been raised in the past two pages. Many questions are raised when we find ourselves sad. Many questions are raised when we experience loss, pain, or stress. Many questions are raised when we shed tears.

So what do we do with all of this?

We find and create spaces where we can carry our questions, our burdens, our storms, and our tears. We carry them to God. We carry them to other caring people.

I carry one simple declaration the speaker made near the end of his talk:

> ***"When you go through it, you will not drown."***

OBEY
{ARMITAGE & ORCHARD}

Winter officially arrived this week. And although it's cold, given the apocalyptic footage of wildfires burning in the mountains of southern California, and the surprising videos of people in southern Louisiana playing in the snow, Chicago was a pretty good place to be this week, weather-wise.

Only a dusting of snow remains of the ground as I drive north along Halsted Street. You have to be a Chicagoan of a certain age to appreciate just how drastic the change has been in the landscape of urban life here.

Not that long ago, this part of the city was home to one of the most notorious housing projects in America: Cabrini-Green.

This morning, as I drive by the sleek glass windows of international schools, boutique clothing stores, upscale movie theaters, bike lanes, and restaurants along Halsted; I can't help but flashback to a time when these blocks were anything but sunny, open, brightly-colored, and inviting.

I thought about the people and families who lived near this stretch of road just one generation ago. I wondered if they could have ever known how valuable their neighborhood would become... once they left.

I cross North Avenue into the theater district, past the Royal George and Steppenwolf. My destination - a large city high school - sits quietly, with a handful of cars parked in its parking lot. Four stone Greek columns frame the facade of the building's front entrance. Colorful banners touting the school's academic programs hang on the outside of the two-story brick structure.

Inside, I pass by a dormant metal detector and I am greeted by a friendly lady who directs me down the hallway towards the auditorium. Tall gray lockers are offset by flags of countries from around the world that are hanging close to the ceiling.

◊

A small greeting table with coffee has been set up at the auditorium entrance. A series of dark curtains partition off the back half of this space. Near the front stage, four singers were warming up with a keyboard player when I entered.

There were only a few people in this section of the auditorium at this point, a few sound and video guys were working on the projection screen. A young man greeted me, and introduced himself.

I wound up having extended conversations with multiple people during my visit.

Later on, the main speaker stood in front of the auditorium's stage and began his talk with a bold statement"

> *"It's a joy to follow God's commands*
> *because we trust his heart.*
> *The reason we trust, love, and obey*
> *is because he has fulfilled*
> *that which was promised."*

There were a lot of potent words in that quote: *joy, follow, commands, trust, love, obey, fulfilled, promised*. Words that we don't often hear used together. For the speaker, obedience to God's commands is the outward expression of a trust-based relationship with God. For the speaker, trust is the inward response to God's kept promises.

Obey is a provocative word. Even writing the word makes me stop and hesitate. Something in me almost instinctively pulls back and says, *'Whoa, hold on a second.'* I'm not sure if this is a product of living at this particular moment in human history, or if it's just a product of being human.

Don't tell me what to do.
Who are you to tell me what to do?
I will do what I want.

For many of us, the word *obey* provokes the schoolyard response: *'Make me.'* For many of us, the word *obedience* provokes a conversation about authority, power, control, force, and pressure.

Most of us obey our society's norms and laws because we have to. Because some person or group of people has the capacity to take things from us, or do harm to us, if we do not comply with their demands. Most of us obey out of fear, or out of a desire to be left alone.

How we understand who or what God is has a huge impact on our views about obedience:

- Is God outside of us, or is God within us?
- If God is outside of us, is God bigger than us? Or all we all equal beings, existing in the universe at the same scale and capacity?
- If God is within us, then shouldn't we have the right to make and obey our own commands, however we see fit?

- Is God an authority figure?
- Is God making laws for humans?
- Is God enforcing laws?
- Is God judging whether the laws were followed?
- Does God care what humans do?
-

The speaker introduced a new frame for thinking about God and obedience:

"God is saying:
I want to help, and let you give up control over your life.
Ultimately, you're a steward, you're not an owner of anything.
I'm humble, but I'm coming to lead.
I'm humble, but I'm coming to direct you."

This is a very different approach to obedience. This is a releasing, a letting go. This is less about giving up and giving in, and more about giving over. The speaker's framing is one of a relationship, a personal relationship, a personal relationship based on trust.

HOLIDAYS
{49TH & KING DRIVE}

The most industrial side street in this city has to be 47th Street. To drive down this street is to pass through a living monument to the part of the city that has manufactured and shipped food, equipment, and materials for the entire country.

I pass by the panel-sided homes of Brighton Park, through the canyons of stacked truck trailers on the pothole-ridden roads surrounding the old stockyards, and through the alternating blocks of renovated buildings and abandoned lots along the southern border of Bronzeville; until I arrive at the proud elegance of the Harold Washington Cultural Center and the stately three-story greystones along this stretch of King Drive.

My destination matches the architectural mood of the confident buildings on this boulevard. The front entrance has the look of an athletic fieldhouse. Its large stone base supports the swooping arched roof which frames the frosted glass windows of the structure's front entrance. An elderly lady in stiletto heels accidentally drops a bracelet. We exchange good morning greetings as I pick it up and hand it to her.

Inside the lobby, two ushers are discussing whether a chair should be placed in front of the auditorium door entrance. I pass them and walk inside the auditorium. The building's arched roof is even more impressive on the inside.

Small groups of people are scattered around the padded seats of this hall, waiting for the event to begin. Most of the people assembled so far are older, many of the women are wearing colorful Sunday hats, many of the men are in suits. An elderly gentleman in a two-piece suit greets me with an extended hand:

..

"Merry Christmas, Seasons Greetings, brother.
Glad to see you. Happy New Year!"

◊

The front stage stands a few steps above the main seating level. Behind the stage, a seating area for the choir rises stadium-style towards a large, colorful, stained glass mural on the wall. The mural contains a few separate, but related, scenes. All the people depicted have a soft brown tint used for their skin.

A speaker came to the podium on the front stage and began the event by declaring to the audience:

"It's good to be here, and it's good to be alive."

The speaker went on to explain that he had been in the hospital for four days during the previous week with a stomach issue. A few minutes later, another speaker came to the podium and shared that he too had recently been hospitalized. In his case, it was the result of side effects from blood pressure medications.

Maybe it's because it is the end of the year, maybe it's because the winter holidays give us time to remember what is truly important to us. Maybe it's because most of us have a visceral reaction to the life-and-death realities of emergency hospital visits. Whatever it is, I zoned out for a few minutes as the first speaker's words played on repeat in my mind.

I snapped out of it as six singers joined the five person band to lead the audience in song, while a 20 person choir began an entrance processional onto the front stage, and up into their seating area. A speaker came to the podium and enthusiastically announced

"It's prayer time. It's prayer time!"

Without any further instructions, audience members made their way to the front stage, forming a line that wrapped around the entire front stage. As I watched them, the older lady sitting in front of me offered her hand, and I noticed other small groups of audience members standing and forming small circles; holding hands and praying together.

This sincere moment of solidarity and community was immediately followed by an energetic one, as the audience members greeted each other and welcomed visitors, including me.

◊

Afterwards, the main speaker came to the podium on the front stage. I knew I was in for a treat when he began his talk with this reflection on the Christmas holiday season:

> *"We get it all twisted regarding what Christmas is about.*
> *Christmas is not about running around*
> *and throwing money all about...*
> *It's about how God has touched our lives*
> *with His love and caring.*
> *We don't care about each other anymore...*
> *It's, 'Look at what I got!'*
> *Our worship life is gone,*
> *our prayer life is in shambles."*

The speaker was continuing a now decades-long post-World War II lamentation by people of faith about the codependency of American consumerism and American Christianity. His words also continue a centuries-long concern that we humans have a habit of forgetting the original intention and meaning behind the rituals, symbols, ceremonies, and holidays we create in the name of God.

The speaker continued:

> *"There must be prayer in our hearts...*
> *Do you hear the cries of the poor?*
> *Tax cuts for the rich?*
> *Healthcare wiped out for the poor?*
> *Lord, do you care?"*

That last line caught me off guard. I was surprised that the speaker's question was directed to God, which is odd considering God was the reason all of us were assembled in this space on this morning.

This has been a year where the question: *"Do you care?!"* has been posed to many prominent individuals in our country. More often than not, the question is rhetorical one, used to mobilize the powerless, and to expose the powerful.

But the speaker was reflecting the genuine cry of all people who find themselves suffering, where the question: *"Lord, do you care?"* is an inquiry. It is full of both hope and despair. It is an awareness that the answer could go either way.

Does God care?
If God cares, why?
If God does not care, why not?
What does God care about?
Who does God care about?
When does God care?

As always, engaging any one of these questions could take an entire book. But we must engage these questions, because the holidays we celebrate today are the result of earlier generations' responses to these questions. And our responses will determine if and/or how we will carry on with the holidays we have, create the holidays we want, or cast aside the holidays we no longer need.

For the speaker, the response is clear:

> *"The Christmas message is that God cares,*
> *and is the same God today*
> *as back then.*
> *God is sending a message*
> *to the hopeless,*
> *to those who have lost heart.*
> *God is sending a message:*
> *There is hope."*

COMPLETION
{56TH & WOODLAWN}

You don't hear birds chirping outside on mornings like this. In this city, the price of a picturesque, snowy Christmas week is single-digit temperatures during the following days. It is cold. The kind of cold that demands silence from nature, and silence was the only thing outside as I walked to my car this morning.

◊

I exit off the Dan Ryan, past the construction equipment along the southern branch of the Green Line, into the quiet and open expanses of Washington Park. The cold air has given the snow a glazed look, and it now reflected even more sunlight than usual.

On the other side of the park, canyons of glass and steel rise between the buildings of the University of Chicago medical center. A glass dome appears on my left. The way the snow is packed at its base, it looks like a spaceship is about to emerge from the ground.

A quick web search reveals that the futuristic structure is a wing of the University's library. One block away, the landscape will transition into the quad lawns and Gothic architecture of the campus center.

◊

My destination matches the stately brick mansions on this stretch of Woodlawn Avenue. Tan brick archways, adorned with Christmas lights and wreaths, form open hallways on either side of the hall. The walls rise to meet a series of large wooden beams, which run from left to right, and form the base of the hall's A-frame ceiling.

A traditional Christmas carol plays from the large organ pipes which hang over the front stage. The beams divide the hall's small frosted stained glass windows into sets of three, each set a different mix of yellow, green, and blue. Yellow globe light bulbs hang from wooden racks on chandeliers connected to the roof by sets of long chains.

Inside, a handful of people are scattered across the padded dark wood benches of the main hall. A man greets me, and two older people in light blue robes smile gently at me, and wish me Happy New Year. A few minutes later, a young woman in a dark robe introduced herself and welcomed me into this space.

The event moves peacefully through a series of organ-backed hymns, poems read by the main speaker, and written meditations which were read aloud in unison by everyone in the hall. The eight-person, blue-robed choir provided musical interludes between the readings from the side of the front stage.

This is the perfect way to end a journey that began 364 days earlier just a few blocks south of this hall. There was no pomp and circumstance. No excessive celebration. It was neither sad and solemn nor angry and bitter.

It was calm. It was grounded. It was rooted in messages of love and peace, with tangible calls to action for all assembled. Reminders of what we can do, what we can control, and what we release to that which is greater than us.

◊

The main speaker came to the front stage and delivered a short talk. She drew inspiration for her words this morning from a verse in the Bible which states: *"The light shines in the darkness, and the darkness has not overcome it*[1]*."*

This verse captures the theme of this book perfectly. There has been no shortage of darkness in Chicago this year. Darkness in individuals, darkness in families, darkness in neighborhoods, darkness in institutions, darkness in leadership, darkness in communities.

The darkness is real. The darkness is powerful. If we look closely, we can see the darkness all around us. If we look even more closely, we can see all the darkness within us.

---

[1] John 1:5

And yet, the light shines. It shines in the people I've seen assemble in buildings large and small across this city. It shines in the voices of the singers who offered their vocal gifts - free of charge - in service to the healing and nourishment of their spiritual neighbors.

The light shines in the words of the speakers who devote their lives to study, prayer, service, and introspection; in the hopes of being useful megaphones through which God can speak to everyday people.

Most importantly, the light shines in those everyday people. The ones I met, and the ones I never will. The everyday people who make a conscious decision, day after day, week after week, to keep connecting with God, and with other people.

The light shines in their struggles, in their scars, in their pains, in their fears, in their cries, in their disappointments. It shines in their small victories, in their fight, in their determination, in their prayers, in their smiles, in their hugs, in their songs, in their children.

"The light shines in the darkness
and the darkness has not overcome it."

The choir descended the short flight of stairs at the base of the front stage, and formed a quiet processional over to the grand piano stationed near the front row of benches. They sang a simple four-line chorus:

Now let us sing with joy and mirth,
Praising the one who gave us birth.
Let every voice rise and attend
to God, whose love shall never end[2].

To everyone who has joined me on this journey:

Here's to you
To your voice rising
To attending to your spirit
To attending your spirit to God, and
To love that does not end.

God Bless.

---

[2] "Now let us sing" Words by John Bell. Copyright©1995 WGRG c/o Iona Community, GIA Publications, Inc., agent. All Rights Reserved. Used by permission.

ACKNOWLEDGEMENTS

The history of this city, like the history of many urban centers in the Northeast and Midwest of the U.S., teaches us that few things are permanent. People migrate, neighborhoods change, buildings are repurposed. What was is not what will be.

We remember the communities and tribes which comprised the Illiniwek confederation, the people who lived on this land 200 years ago, the people for whom the state of Illinois is named.

We remember the Haitian-born, Black man of African and French ancestry who is credited with constructing the first permanent settlement in the area that would become Chicago.

We remember the immigrants from around the world who transformed this town into a metropolis, and constructed majestic structures to celebrate their God and to care for their souls.

I remember my parents who, at the time of my birth, were residents of Chicago by way of Nigeria; who were starting a new family in a new city in a new country; and whose complete dependence on God can only be understood by those who know what it's like to be far from home.

I remember the American descendants of enslaved Africans, who migrated en masse from the terror of the South and encountered a new kind of trouble in the North; whose pain and promise nourished one Thomas Andrew Dorsey, a resident of Chicago by way of Georgia, and the godfather of gospel music. I have found community and comfort in the spaces they created for their spiritual and psychological nourishment. I am humbled by the generosity and openness they have shown to this *brotha' from another mother*. Their existence and resistance in this place is a demonstration of the inextinguishable light of God that resides within all of us.

I remember the families from other countries, cultures, and communities who have joined in the joyful work of creating Dr. King's beloved community here on Earth, at intersections across this city.

I remember the families who have been deemed *white*, yet have chosen to use their priority status in this city - and in our society - to elevate the concerns and contributions of humans who inhabit other bodies.

I remember the following institutions I visited during 2017 while writing this book. I am inspired by people who, in a world of seemingly endless options, chose to stay, to sow, and to see the harvest. They didn't know I was coming. They didn't know I would write about my experience when I left. They knew their space should be open to all who seek God, and it is because of their obedience and openness that this project exists. Thank you, and Thank God.

ACKNOWLEDGEMENTS

Listed in the order I visited them:

Apostolic Church of God *(63rd & Dorchester)*
Lawndale Christian Community Church *(Ogden & Avers)*
Fellowship Missionary Baptist Church *(45th & Princeton)*
New Life Community Church Midway *(51st & Keeler)*
Mars Hill Baptist Church of Chicago *(Austin & Lake)*
Trinity United Church of Christ *(95th & Eggleston)*
Rock of Our Salvation Church *(Washington & Parkside)*
Salem Baptist Church of Chicago *(114th & Corliss)*
Armitage Baptist Church *(Kedzie & Albany)*
Progressive Baptist Church of Chicago *(37th & Wentworth)*
River City Community Church *(Grand & Hamlin)*
Saint Sabina Church *(78th & Racine)*
United Baptist Church *(Roosevelt & Tripp)*
CityPoint Community Church *(23rd & Michigan)*
Canaan Community Church *(Garfield & Paulina)*
Holy Trinity Church Downtown *(Wabash & Erie)*
Apostolic Faith Church *(38th & Indiana)*
The Moody Church *(Clark & LaSalle)*
Redeemer Church - Chicago *(North & Rutherford)*
St. Stephen AME Church *(Washington & Albany)*
Chicago Tabernacle *(Cicero & Belmont)*
Quinn Chapel AME Church *(24th & Wabash)*
Soul City Church *(Racine & Adams)*
Friendship Baptist Church *(Jackson & Laramie)*
Edgewater Baptist Church *(Hollywood & Glenwood)*
Carter Temple CME Church *(79th & Wabash)*
New Mt. Pilgrim MB Church *(Washington & Kildare)*
Jesus House Chicago *(Kedzie & Montrose)*
City Church Chicago *(Chicago & Green)*
Greater St. John AME Church *(62nd & Throop)*
Oasis Church Chicago *(Cermak & Canalport)*
Christ Bible Church *(79th & Coles)*
Second City Church *(Armitage & Orchard)*
Liberty Baptist Church *(49th & King Drive)*
Hyde Park Union Church *(56th & Woodlawn)*

Made in the USA
Las Vegas, NV
11 January 2023